The Bible,
Fact or
Fiction?

Exciting and Compelling
Facts to Consider

Lynnette Lloyd

Outskirts Press, Inc.
Denver, Colorado

Scripture References
All scripture is taken from the Holy Bible versions:
(NKJV) New King James Version, Thomas Nelson Publisher Study Bible, copyright 1997 by Thomas Nelson, Inc. Used by permission.
(NASB) New American Standard Bible, Copyright 1960, 1962, 1963, 1968, 1971, 1972, 1973, 1975 1977, 1995 by the Lockman Foundation. Used by Permission.

The opinions expressed in this manuscript are solely the opinions of the author and do not represent the opinions or thoughts of the publisher. The author has represented and warranted full ownership and/or legal right to publish all the materials in this book.

Outskirts Press, Inc.
http://www.outskirtspress.com

ISBN: 978-1-4327-2342-2

Outskirts Press and the "OP" logo are trademarks belonging to Outskirts Press, Inc.

PRINTED IN THE UNITED STATES OF AMERICA

Table of Contents

Life - Is This All There Is?

Where are you in life right now? Happy? Sad? Lonely? Feeling rejected, loved or betrayed? Overworked, under-worked? Happily married, unhappily married, divorced, single? Young, old, rich, poor? What season of life are you in?

Do you ever ask, "Why am I here?" or What is the meaning of life, specifically in my life? Is there a purpose to life? Does it even matter what I do? And when I am done prodding through this life, then what? Is this it? Is this all there is?

Life is hard, and the world we live in can be dismal, scary and foreboding with all the war, nuclear issues, global issues, moral issues and terrorist attacks. Many wonder is there an end and how will it all end?

I think everyone in his or her life has at some point or another felt several of these emotions and has had these questions. I know I have.

Wherever you are in life, this book is for you. Life is a journey that we know very little about, but you will be amazed at what you learn in this book about life, this planet, this universe, your purpose and what to expect after this life. **In fact, you will be amazed at how much there really is to life-and how just existing in this universe is miraculous.**

The four main questions we will be examining are:

1. Where did we come from?

Credit: Nasa, ESA &Hubble Heritage Team (STScI/Aura)

2. Why and how did we get here?

NASA — Ib.

3. What is the purpose of my life?

?

4. Where will I go after I die?

Introduction

But where do we find the answers and how do we know what is truth? We may search for the answers by looking at the facts of science and by looking at different philosophies, theories and religions. If we narrowed down the extensive research in these different areas to a quick, simple synopsis, how would they stack up with science, astronomy, history, archaeology, physics and logic? Most people look in the following areas to find the answers, therefore, that is where we will look to see which one supports the most facts and evidence.

Evolution
The Big Bang Theory
Creationism
Science, History
Religions – Different ones
Witchcraft, Satanism
The Bible

You, like a juror sitting in the juror's box will be able to sift through the evidence of **where the truth lines up with the facts** substantiating and even contributing to science, astronomy, history, archaeology, medicine and even prophecies with 100% accuracy.

Neither you nor I have time to waste on a fairy tale, we are only interested in the facts. So, I will present this information to you in a simple and logical format, and let you make your own conclusions, regarding the age old questions, "Where did I come from? Why am I here? What is my purpose? and Where will I go after I die?

There is so much more you can discover in your own research, and hopefully this will wet your appetite to seek out more in-depth data on these issues. For simplicity, I will only list a few examples in each category and as time permits you can research more via the listed resources or the internet. <u>This is exciting stuff</u> and I hope you enjoy reading it as much as I enjoyed researching it and sharing it with you!

In order to find out where the answers to life lie and the purpose to why you are here, it would be helpful to ponder some facts all around us in science, astronomy, history and archaeology to find these answers that are out there for anyone willing to take the time to research them.

This Unique Planet and You

Chapter 1

Astronomy, Science & Physics Facts

Part A. OUR PLANET AND THE UNIVERSE

 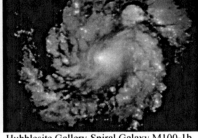

Credit: JPL/NASA 1a.   Hubblesite Gallery-Spiral Galaxy M100-1b.

How did we get here? There are only two answers to choose from:

1.) By Intelligent Design or
2.) By Chance

In researching these two origins of how we got here, we can deduce our purpose, or lack of, for why we are here. If we find we are here by "Intelligent Design" we can reasonably surmise a purpose for existing and being here.

3

If, on the other hand, we conclude that we got here by chance (evolution or an explosion) then we will realize we have no real purpose for being here and what we do or do not do will have little or no consequence.

First and foremost it is important to note that it is an understatement to say <u>we are special in the universe.</u> Our planet earth is a unique pale dot in the cosmic sea! We are the only known planet in the entire universe that has complex life and that makes you and I special. We are one of more than 100 billion galaxies in the universe. In fact, scientists say they don't even know how big the expanse of the universe is. Does this sphere exist for a purpose? Do you know how big our universe is? According to Wikipedia, typical galaxies contain ten million to one trillion (10^7 to 10^{12}) stars, all orbiting a common center of gravity. Astronomers say that our Milky Way has from between 400 million stars to possibly two billion stars. Now through the high tech telescopes, we have been able to find 100 billion other galaxies all with 200-400 million stars and there could be 1 trillion galaxies. According to Dr. Van Impe, if one could travel 700 million miles per hour, it would take 10 billion years to cross our universe! Most galaxies are several thousand to several hundred thousand light years in diameter and are usually separated from one another by distances on the order of millions of light years. (A light year is the distance light can travel in one year, which is 9,500,000,000,000 kilometers. A kilometer is 1000 meters or 0.6214 miles.) Check out Nasa's website to see how incredibly beautiful and vast it is up there.

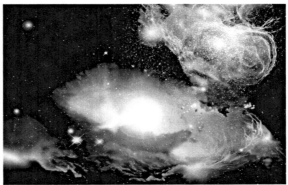

Credit: NASA/ESA/ESO/Wolfram Freudling et al. (STECF)

As H.M.S. Richards writes in *Fireworks in the Sky*, "For all our vaunted knowledge, we are just a speck of dust in an infinite cosmos." What holds the earth in its orbit around the sun? What causes it to spin on its axis? What keeps the moon out there whirling about the earth century after century? The earth is flying on a path around the sun at a rate of 66,000 miles an hour. There is nothing haphazard about the universe. Starting with the earth, we can project ourselves to the infinitely large or to the infinitely small, and everywhere we look we see intelligent design. The earth swings in its path around the sun, following exact laws.

1c.

The sun moves about the center of our vast galaxy, controlled by those same intricate and complex laws.

Equally exact and complex in design are the molecules, the atoms, the electrons, neutrons, protons (the world of the infinitely small). We live in a universe so marvelous, so breathtaking, and so beautiful."

An interesting side note is, when most of us think we aren't moving at all, perhaps sleeping, we are actually traveling at a faster speed than jets which travel at approximately 570 mph. We are minute by minute, even in our sleep, traveling at 1,110 miles every minute, or 66,600 miles an hour. How fast is that? About thirty times faster than a speeding bullet. Did you realize that even when you are standing still, you are actually traveling faster than a speeding bullet? Yet, we don't even feel it. How can that be?

In the DVD, "The Privileged Planet" it states, "Location is everything for sustaining life and the privilege to be able to scientifically view discoveries in the skies. Gravity pulls matter together and without any one of these primary laws, we could not exist. A strong nuclear force holds electrons, protons and neutrons together. All these laws must be in place to have life! The universe is finely tuned with:

Gravity force

Electronic force

Strong nuclear force

If even one of these changed by just a minor amount we could not exist!"

Again, our position in the universe is unique. Think about it —most people know very little about it, much less understand it. Yet our planet and the universe is so complex that it stands to reason that superior intelligence had to have been involved to create and sustain our universe. How could some explosion billions of years ago create and maintain such order and complexity? Who is behind all this brilliance? The universe is so huge that scientists don't know where it ends and they tell us there is no planet like ours. If we haven't seen already, we are beginning to see that ours is a special planet and we are a special creation, created by an awesome Creator!

We are positioned just right in the universe for a multitude of life sustaining formulas. For instance, the earth is positioned in exactly the right place for the exact proportion of the gravitational pull of the moon that we need for certain things such as cleaning our continents and harbors and seashores by the ocean tides.

Mass and Size of the Earth

Like the story of the three bears, conditions for life on earth are just right! Not too cold, not too hot, not too close, not too far away, not too big, not too small but just right. Most people don't realize how complex and miraculous it is just to be surviving in this universe and on this planet. The only planet known to have life.

1. Earth is just the right size. If the earth were 10% larger or 10% smaller than it is, life would not be possible on this planet!

2. It is just the right distance from the sun so that we receive just the right amount of heat and light. If the earth were farther away from the sun we would freeze and if it were closer to the sun (such as the distance of Mercury or Venus) we would burn up.

3. The tilt of the axis of the earth is 23 degrees.

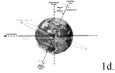

1d.

Isn't it interesting that there is a tilt to the ground we stand on, yet we don't feel disoriented? This tilt rotates at such a degree as to ensure that the earth is slowly turned in all parts of its surface before the rays of the sun. If there were no tilt to the axis, the poles would accumulate enormous masses of ice, and the center part of the earth would become intensely hot.[1]

The Moon

1e.

Another amazing aspect of our solar system is our moon. Did you know that it would be impossible to live on the earth without the moon? The moon cleans up the oceans and shores of all our continents which is done by the tides. Without the tides, created by the moon, all harbors and shores would be a cesspool of garbage. The tides continuously break upon the shores, aerating the oceans of this planet and providing plankton, which is the very foundation of the food chain. Without the plankton, there would be no oxygen and man would not be able to live on earth.[2]

The moon is just the right size and the exact distance from the earth to perform numerous strategic functions for life on planet earth. Although the earth needs the moon, the moon cannot sustain life and is in fact dangerous to humans without necessary space equipment to survive. For instance, the moon has no air, no atmosphere, no oxygen.

No atmosphere means no air molecules to scatter the light so the sky is always dark. The temperature on the moon goes from an extreme 270 degrees below zero at night to a whopping 270 degrees above zero during the day. Humans must wear space equipment to survive. (You can read more about this in NASA's website.)

While most of us are oblivious to the dynamics and miraculous pinpoint continuous activity going on all around us in the unseen realm, something or someone is keeping it all going. Did you know that if even one of the chemicals or dynamics were off, we couldn't survive?

<u>The Atmosphere</u>

Even though you can't see the air that we breathe or the atmosphere all around us, we must have it to survive. A thin layer of atmosphere surrounds the earth. We live under a great ocean of air – 78% nitrogen, 21% oxygen and 1% of almost a dozen different trace elements. **No other planet** in the known universe is made up of this mixture of atmosphere. These elements are not chemically combined but are <u>continually</u> mixed mechanically by the tidal effect of the moon upon the atmosphere. This has the same effect that it has upon the seas and always provides the same amount of oxide into the atmosphere which is absorbed into the ocean which allows people to be able to continue to live on this planet. If the atmosphere were not as thick as it is, we would be crushed by the billion pieces of cosmic debris and meteorites which fall continually into our atmosphere.[3]

Because our atmosphere has the exact proportions of chemicals that it does, we are the only planet with complex life that can look out past our planet and see what is out there. It's like something or someone wanted us to be able to explore more out there and understand more of the creator. We have less than 1 percent of carbon dioxide which makes our atmosphere transparent, whereas the other five planets in our solar system have an atmosphere with too much carbon dioxide, thus creating a milky cloudiness and therefore cannot see past their planet, even if they could sustain complex life.

The rarity of our complex life-sustaining atmosphere, and position in the universe with all the dangers such as black holes, gravity or lack of, positions in relation to the sun and moon need a whole book to explain the miracles needed to sustain our complex earth and its surroundings.

The Ozone Layer

Forty miles up, there is a thin layer of ozone. If compressed it would only be a quarter of an inch thick, and yet without ozone life could not exist.[4]

Water

There is nowhere else in the universe that we find water in any abundance except here on the earth. Water, the amazing solvent, dissolves almost everything upon this earth except those things which are life sustaining. This amazing liquid exists as ice, breaks up rocks and produces soil. As snow, it stores up water in the valleys. As rain, it waters and cleanses the earth. As vapor, it provides moisture for much of the arable land of this earth. It exists as cloud cover, in just the right amount. If we had clouds like Venus, Earth could not exist. We have exactly 50 percent of the surface of the earth covered by clouds at any one time, allowing just the right amount of sunlight to come through.[5]

Dust

Did you know that dust provides an incredible function for mankind? If it were not for dust, we would never see a blue sky. Seventeen miles above this planet there is no dust from the earth, and the sky is always black. If it were not for dust, it would never rain. One drop of rain is made up of eight million minuscule droplets of water, and each one of those eight million droplets is wrapped around a tiny particle of dust. Without these, the world would become parched and life would cease to exist.[6]

How Did the Universe Begin?

Where and how did the universe begin? Some say a big bang exploded and created all this miraculous life bearing cosmos and earth into this organized system that sustains life in our universe and on our planet. Others say it was evolution and still others say it had to be an intelligent Master Designer or Creator. As we have seen, and logic tells us, explosions cause chaos, not order. Just as we know a building has to have an architect, and a car needs a designer and manufacturer, a watch was engineered, and even something as simple as a mousetrap had to have someone design it and make it, yet if even one component is missing in something as simple as a mousetrap, it wouldn't work. Think about it. From a pencil

11

to a mousetrap, to a light bulb, to a car, to a city, someone had to create and build them. We can see the dynamics and tools we need to create these material things but who truly comprehends all the dynamics of the earth floating in space in the vast universe with so many intricate details? Scientists and astronomers alike will tell you they don't understand it all.

Science, Astronomy, Medicine and the Bible

Check out the facts in the following spreadsheet prepared by Ray Comfort comparing what the Bible had to say scientifically, astronomically, and medically over 2000 years ago and how it took science years to catch up with what the Bible stated before the advanced ages of science, medicine and astronomy.

SCIENCE CONFIRMS THE BIBLE

THE BIBLE 2,000-3,000 yrs ago	Science Then	Science Now
The earth is a sphere. (Isaiah 40:22)	The earth was a flat disk.	The earth is a sphere.
Innumerable stars. (Jeremiah 33:22)	Only 1,100 stars.	Innumerable stars.
Free float of earth in space. (Job 26:7)	Earth sat on a large animal.	Free float of earth in space.
Creation made of invisible elements. (Hebrews 11:3)	Science was ignorant on the subject.	Creation made of invisible elements (atoms).
Each star is different. (1 Cor. 15:41).	All stars were the same.	Each star is different.
Light moves (Job 38:19,20)	Light was fixed in place.	Light moves.
Air has weight. (Job 28:25)	Air was weightless.	Air has weight.
Blood is the source of life & health. (Leviticus 17:11)	Sick people must be bled. (i.e. G. Washington)	Blood is the source of life & health.
Ocean floor contains deep valleys & mntns (2 Sam. 22:16; Jonah 2:6).	The ocean floor was flat.	Ocean floor contains deep valleys and mountains.
When dealing with disease, hands should be washed under running water. (Lev. 15:13).	Hands washed in still water (caused thousands of deaths by infection)	When dealing with disease, hands should be washed under running water.

Used by permission. Ray Comfort, The Believers Evidence Bible

Let's just review a few of these spreadsheet facts:

1. ₁g. <u>The earth is a sphere</u>
At a time when science believed that the earth was flat, it was the Scriptures that inspired Christopher Columbus to sail around the world. Remember until 1492 everyone, including scientists, thought the world was flat and people would sail right off of it. While everyone was believing the world was flat, the Bible stated in Isaiah 40:22, "The earth is a sphere." It is important to note that scholars say the book of Isaiah was written approximately 700 B.C.

2. ₁h. <u>Innumerable Stars-can't be counted.</u>
How could anyone on this earth know how many stars were out in space before the telescopes? The first telescope wasn't invented until about 1608. Yet the Bible says in the book of Jeremiah and Genesis 15:5 there were so many stars that you couldn't count them. (These scriptures were written over 3000 years ago.)

In 128 B.C. Hippicause declared there were 1026 stars. In 150 A.D. Ptolemy said there were 1056 stars. In 1575 A.D. Tyco Brahe said there were 777 stars. For years scientists were counting and classifying certain numbers of stars around a 1000 or less. In 1627 the noted astronomer Johannes Kepler published a catalog showing a total of 1,005 stars.

Fact: Science now attests to what the Bible declared

14

over 3000 years ago. Interesting isn't it? You can read any current astronomy book and learn there are so many stars we can't count them.

3. Free float of the Earth

The earth hangs on nothing. The Bible says in Job 26:7, "He spreads out the northern skies, over empty space; He suspends the earth over nothing." At the time that the books of the Old Testament were written, the world was in a state of ignorance. People believed (incorrectly) that the world was flat. But something had to hold up the flat earth. In mythology, we find the flat earth being held up on the shoulders of Atlas. Hindus believed that four huge elephants were holding up the four corners of the earth. In other cultures, pillars of stone were the foundation (although what they or the elephants or Atlas stood on was somehow never discussed.) And as far as "How did the earth get here?" Outside of the Bible were different ideas ranging from the earth being a very large egg, laid in some cultures by the Big Bird Goddess, on others by the Crocodile Life Giver. But the Bible states in the book of Genesis, "In the beginning God created the heavens and the earth." Genesis 1:1. According to the Bible, in the book of Job 26:7, (which was written over 3,500 years ago) it says "He (God) stretches out the north over empty space; He hangs the earth on nothing." Nothing! How could they possibly comprehend this fact? Even we, who live in a highly technical scientific age, know very little about the cosmos. How heavy is this earth that hangs on nothing and continually turns to the light while just being suspended? Scientists have computed the earth to weigh 6,592,000,000,000,000,000,000, tons. That is 6.5 sextillion tons.

15

Can you conceive the power that enables this earth to float lightly through space, keeping perfect time in its race around the sun? Not only is the earth invisibly supported in space, it is performing a whole series of complicated movements spinning, whirling, through space. It turns on its own axis; it revolves around the sun in its 584 million-mile trip; and in its colossal orbit in our own home galaxy it speeds along at 155 miles a second.[7] According to Wikipedia, the orbital speed of the earth averages about 67,000 miles per hour. (Taking several factors into account such as orbit around the sun, orbiting in our galaxy, makes range of speed between 66,000-67,000 mph.) Amazing, isn't it? Stop for a moment and try to comprehend these facts! Kind of dizzying, isn't it?

4. <u>Creation made of invisible atoms.</u>

Only in recent years has science discovered that everything we see is composed of invisible atoms. Yet, the Bible says in Hebrews 11:3, "By faith we understand that the universe was formed at God's command, so that what is seen was not made out of what was visible."

Credit: Nasa

Science expresses the universe in five terms: time, space, matter, power, and motion. Genesis 1:1, 2 states such truths. In the beginning (time) God created (power) the heaven (space) and the earth (matter)…And the Spirit of God moved (motion) upon the face of the waters. From the first beginning God tells man that He, God, controls all forces of the universe. Oh, and did you know that the atmosphere has incredible weight? Back in the Middle Ages scholars argued the possibility that air could even have weight, opposed to the idea. In the Bible, Job 28:23-25, says"…for God looks to the ends of the earth, and sees under the whole heavens, to establish a weight for the wind and measures the waters." Again, finally science has caught up and the latest text on astronomy declares that the weight of the earth's atmosphere is over 6 quadrillion tons. That's a 6 followed by 15 zeros. Why aren't we crushed?

Blood is the source of life

And one last fact from our spreadsheet: Blood being the source of life. The truth concerning the importance of blood in our body was not fully comprehended until recent years. Up until 120 years ago, sick people were bled (blood was drained from the body), and many died because of this practice, including George Washington who in 1799 was bled (his veins were cut to drain out the supposed bad blood) and he died as a result of the procedure. Yet over 3000 years ago the Bible says in Leviticus 17:11, "For the life of a creature is in the blood…" declaring that the source of life is in the blood. Amazing!

We see that accuracy in science did not come before the Bible, but that science is catching up with the Bible, and we will also see this in astronomy, archaeology, history, and prophecy.

Though we have only looked at a few amazing facts

regarding existence on planet earth, we see amazing detail given to supporting life. In beginning our study on the two main theories of how we got here and how life is continually sustained, is there evidence that we got here by an explosion, or by adaptation, survival of the fittest, or will the facts above support intelligent design and in doing so show the importance of human life, how we got here, why we are here and where will we go next? We will study more on the origin of the universe and life in Chapter 2.

Part B. THE HUMAN BODY

What makes humans so special? Again, we will only be reviewing a small list of the incredible miracles of (just) being alive.

The Brain   1i.

Weighing about 3.3 pounds, the brain can perform what 500 tons of electrical and electronic equipment cannot do. Containing at least 12 billion neurons intertwined with 100 trillion connections, it performs feats that absolutely…well-- boggle the mind! Emil Borel, the great French scientist and probability expert, points out that if anything on the cosmic level is of a probability ration of more than 10^{50} to 1, it will never happen. The probability of producing a human cell by chance is $10^{119,000}$ to 1, -----a number we cannot even comprehend. According to probability scientists, it could never happen. As stated earlier, the human brain has 12 billion brain cells intertwined with 100 trillion connections, how does evolution account for this?

From disorder to order?[9] To illustrate a number as large as 100 trillion, molecular biologist Michael Denton suggests visualizing a solid forest of trees covering half the United States. If each tree contains one hundred thousand leaves, the connections in a human brain would equal the total number of leaves in the entire forest. We generally associate complexity with intelligence. Dr. Carolyn Leaf, specializing in brain research, states "at any one moment, your brain is creatively performing about 400 billion actions, of which you are only conscious of around 2000." The more complex a building or machine, the more intelligence is required for it be engineered. Even if communication engineers could apply the most sophisticated engineering techniques known to humanity, the assembly of an object remotely resembling the human brain would require an eternity of time. Even then they still wouldn't know where to begin. The human brain is unique.

What causes mankind to transcend the animal world and probe space, develop computers, discover DNA, and create art and music? What makes us unique? The answer comes down to three pounds of lumpy gray matter floating around in our heads. Nothing else in the universe, even remotely approaches the complexity of the human brain. The ability to speak distinguishes man from the entire ape family. Although human beings have both the hardware and the software for language, apes don't. For speech to work, the brain structure, the tongue, the larynx, and the vocal cords, and many other parts all need to be fully developed.

Humans have the ability to conceptualize,

resulting in the development of art, literature, mathematics and science. Animals lack this unique human quality.[9]

The Eye 1j.

Then there is the wonder of wonders: The human eye! How could anybody look at a human eye and suppose that it just happened? Imagine creating two eyes on a horizontal plane so that we not only can see but we also have a range finder that determines distances.

Sir Charles Scott Sherrington, famous English physiologist of Oxford, who wrote a classic work on the eye, said: "Behind the intricate mechanism of the human eye lie breath-taking glimpses of a Master Plan." When confronted with darkness, the human eye increases its ability to see one hundred thousand times. The finest camera ever made does not even vaguely approach such a thing, but the human eye does it automatically. Furthermore, the eye will find the object it wants to see and focus on it automatically. It will elongate or compress itself. Both eyes moving together must take different angles to fix themselves upon what is to be seen. Our eyes are built beneath a bony ridge for protection and a nose on which to hang the glasses that most of us need, as well as a shutter for protection from any foreign object.[10]

Each human eye…

- Has over 100 million rods
- Handles 1.5 million simultaneous messages
- Moves 100,000 times each day
- Has automatic focusing

- Has six million cones
- Can distinguish among seven million colors.[11]

How could this be chance? How could some chaotic blast create such precision? There had to be a master designer! Charles Darwin said, "To suppose that the eye could have been formed by natural selection, seems, I freely confess, absurd in the highest degree."

One more important detail about the eye. The eye must connect to the brain somehow. Just as there is no actual input without the keyboard being attached to the computer,

sight is not sight without a brain to receive it. But how does the eye know where the brain is, or what a brain is, or that it even exists; or that it is required to make the eye useful? And how did the eye then wire itself to the brain? Why did it not connect itself to the nose or to the knee? And even if it knew to connect to the brain properly (a feat in itself) how did the eye know how to speak a language the brain would understand and vice versa? Again we need a language created prior to and apart from the existence of the things that will speak the language. And again, an intelligent designer is the best explanation. The eye could not have self-directed or self-organized.[12]

The Heart 1k.

Depending on the activity level, the human heart beats over seventy times a minute, 100,000 times a day for 365 days a year, year after year which results in moving over seven tons of blood through the body's 60,000 plus blood vessels. Amazingly, while the heart is doing all this activity, it is not working hard. It is capable of doing much more. For example, while a person is exercising, the heart can actually double the amount of blood pumped with each beat by greatly speeding up its pumping rate by up to 220 beats a minute.

The six quarts of blood that each adult has are made up of over 24 trillion cells that are pumped by the heart throughout the body making three to five thousand trips every day! During an average lifetime, the heart consistently and automatically (thank goodness) pumps 53 million gallons of blood.

Our Blood

Within human beings there are many things that tell us we must have had a Creator. Our life is based upon the blood that flows in our veins. The amazing blood cell, created in the bone marrow, immediately gives up its nucleus when it reaches the bloodstream. For any other cell, this would mean death, like cutting the heart right out of a man. A blood cell is formed like a doughnut with a thin membrane across the hole. Without a nucleus it is able to carry more oxygen for the body because of this membrane and the shape of the cell. If it were shaped like other cells, it would require nine times as many cells to provide oxygen for the human body.[14]

The Cell

What goes on in a cell is phenomenal. Carl Sagen states, "In the simplest cell we have information equivalent of 10 to the 12th bits, (comparable to 100 million pages of Encyclopedia Britannica.) How could this just happen randomly? Charles Darwin, founder of evolution stated that the cell was simple. Quite the opposite is true.

Though we cannot see a cell without a microscope, what goes on in a cell is astounding! Cells are the basic building blocks of your body. The wisdom in each cell is said to exceed all the accumulated knowledge of the entire human race. No one on earth can explain what makes an individual cell operate.

The cell is the site of more chemical reactions than all the chemical factors in the world combined. The cell, with its thousands of components, chromosomes, genes, DNA, organelles, hormones, enzymes, amino acids and thousands of various chemicals and compounds can be studied, but the force behind these functions is far beyond our comprehension. Amazingly, though you cannot see them, scientists estimate your body is made up of 75 trillion cells. They are so tiny you would need 10,000 to cover a pinhead and yet these cells can operate with pinpoint accuracy for 100 years!

Inside the cells is DNA. DNA is what determines your hair and eye color, gender and the fragrance of a flower. Although thousands of cells die and are replaced everything three seconds, if you took the DNA from all the genes of all the cells in your body, seventy-five trillion, they would fit into the size of an ice-cube, yet stretched out and unwound the string would stretch almost eighty billion miles.

Body Temperature and Food Transformation

The body must generate and maintain a constant temperature at about 98.6 degrees while performing all of its millions of functions. Our skin, the biggest organ of the body, is made up of over 4 million pores that are constantly acting as the cooling system for this machine. The food we eat is transformed from the digestive and metabolic systems into healthy blood, bone and cell structure. The lungs succeed in supplying the blood with the oxygen it needs.

Overall Body

The human body and the immense intelligence that directs it is unmatched in power, intelligence, and adaptability. We humans take for granted the millions of functions we perform simultaneously every day and yet the inherent intelligence directing and enabling us is absolutely staggering. Think of the adaptability of mind and body. Ponder for a moment just how adaptable our bodies really are. Imagine yourself paying your bills while simultaneously watching a movie and surfing the web for a research project. How well will you perform these three functions? Probably not too well. Now, at the same time, vacuum the floors, bake cookies and prepare dinner. Trying to do those six tasks at the same time leaves no chance for any of them to be performed well, and that is only six activities. Twenty four hours a day your body is performing quadrillions of processes! Not millions, billions or even trillions, but quadrillions and even more incredible is how our bodies perform all these functions with pinpoint perfection. The enormous intelligence directing our bodies is extraordinarily amazing.

Reproduction and Miscellaneous Body Functions

No other machine can reproduce itself like the incredible human body. It really is incomprehensible and miraculous that a fertilized ovum can and does turn into a fully grown man or woman.

George Gallup, the famous statistician, said, "I could prove God statistically; take the human body alone, the chance that all the functions of the individual would just happen, is a statistical monstrosity."

The human body is incredibly complex. You could spend years studying the different functions of the body, but since most of us are short on time, a good resource to read to get a quick synopsis on many of the amazing feats of the human body is www.creationresearch/body.

Scientists and Creationists

One last fact regarding science. It is a fact that most of the great scientists who founded and developed the key issues of science were creationists! Research the following list of renown scientists:

Physics: Newton, Faraday, Maxwell, Kelvin
Chemistry: Boyle, Dalton Pascal, Ramsay
Biology: Ray, Linnaeus, Mendel, Pasteur
Astronomy: Kepler, Galileo, Herschel

These highly recognized scientists are among many who were creationists, not evolutionists.

Now, speaking of evolution, let's move on to Chapter 2 and check out some facts regarding evolution and the big bang theory.

Where Did We Come From?

Theories of Evolution, the Big Bang or a Master Designer?

Chapter 2

Evolution and the Big Bang Theory

Basically, there are two views on how the universe began: spontaneously or by design. It has to be one or the other and therefore, we need to look at both views in order to draw a conclusion.

Part A: Evolution – Fact or Fiction?

2a.

The theory of evolution really took hold in 1840 with the published book by Charles Darwin, called "The Evolution of the Species." Then in 1912, a lawyer by the name of Charles Dawson announced his discovery of pieces of a human skull and an apelike jaw in a gravel pit near the town of Piltdown, England. Experts (incorrectly) declared Piltdown Man estimated to be 300,000 to one million years old. They thought Darwin's missing link had been found. This mistake continued for 40 years until 1953 when Piltdown man was found out to be a hoax. Radiocarbon tests proved that its skull belonged to a 600-year old woman, and its jaw to a 500 year old orangutan from the East Indies. (Our Time: The Illustrated History of the 20th Century) Also see Wikipedia on the internet for more information on this hoax and the article of other hoaxes and mistakes undermining the credibility of evolutionists.

The Piltdown Man fraud was not an isolated incident. The famed Nebraska Man was derived from a single tooth, which was later found to be from an extinct pig. Java Man, found in the early 20th century was nothing more than a piece of skull, a fragment of a thigh bone, and three molar teeth. The rest came from the deeply fertile imaginations of plaster of Paris workers. Java Man is now regarded as fully human. The Neanderthal Man was exposed as being fully human, not an ape.[1] You can research the results of these and more evolution hoaxes on the internet under any of their names, i.e. Java Man, Nebraska Man, Peking Man, etc or Google www.wikipedia/nebraskaman, or any of the above.

Scores of archaeologists, scientists, and others have spent centuries trying to disprove and show discrepancies and errors in the Bible, (some of which will be discussed in the Historical and Archaeological chapter), but they have not been able to disprove its claims. Imagine if the Bible had made false claims like evolutionists, they would have been exposed and the world would know about them. Why is evolution still being taught as fact? Darwin himself never claimed evolution to be a fact; he said it was a theory. Why then should science? Darwin thought that through time we would eventually find the missing links. After all these years they are STILL MISSING! If evolution is true there should be thousand of transitions. Evolution requires intermediate forms between species. But there are none. Not a single instance. Some of the greatest scientists in the world look upon evolution as something absolutely absurd, impossible and improvable. See DissentFromDarwin.org. Clearly, if evolution were indeed a fact, then the fossil records should shout it to the world. But the truth is that they do not.

Darwin's theory also says that complex creatures evolve from simple creatures naturally over time. Science teaches in the Second Law of Thermodynamics that things tend to move from a state of order to disorder. In other words, things tend to decay over time, not improve over time. This goes against the theory of evolution which teaches that things and creatures evolved from simplicity to complexity. Though we are usually taught in school that we evolved from apes, I recently sat in the Smithsonian's Evolution room and watched a movie showing that according to evolution we originally came from a rodent, they call Grandma Morgie. I was so taken aback that I had to sit through the movie twice, because I could hardly believe what I was hearing. First of all, it is obvious humans are so much more intelligent than rodents and apes and secondly, if we evolved from a rodent or an ape for reasons of survival of the fittest, why are there still apes and rodents and people all at the same time? Darwin, himself stated that this theory is not a fact, just a theory. Darwin also stated in 1905, "Not one change of species into another is on record...we cannot prove that a single species has been changed." (Charles Darwin, My Life & Letters Vol. 1 Page 210, 1905)

The theory of evolution tells us that the species that existed are by survival of the fittest. Evolutionists believe that it takes millions of years for things to adapt to their environment and that those individuals which best adapted survived while those which did not died out. But if the survival of the fittest determined the type of life forms now existing in the world today, then in each species only the best suited would have survived. We should have a bird, a fish, a reptile, a cat, a plant, etc.

There are 625,000 different kinds of insects. There are 12,000 different species of mammals, 340,000 of birds, 40,000 of fish. Over 5,000 different species of reptiles.

For fun reading, read a few of these facts regarding evolutionary problems from, "A Scientific Approach to Christianity" by Robert Faid. Remember evolution teaches that adaptation took millions of years to transpire and so the question to ask is, "How did living creatures survive while waiting for the adaptations needed?

➢ 2b 2c. Evolutionists tell us that birds have evolved from fish, and that the wings of birds are adaptations of fish fins. But let us examine these two appendages. The fin of a fish is hard and rigid. The bones of a fish are heavy, including the structure of the spiny portion of the fin. The reason that the bones of a fish are heavy is that a fish must live under water. The fish must have a specific gravity greater than water or he would float on the surface. On the other hand, a bird's bones are hollow, including those in the wing. The bird must be as light as possible in order to fly. Just as the heavy, rigid fin of the fish is engineered to push against the heavy forces of water, the wings of a bird are engineered to give sufficient strength with a minimum of weight for the bird to fly in the air. Just what good would a partially developed fin or gill be to a fish? What happened to the hypothetical missing link when he possessed a half fin-half wing appendage? It would not have been able to either swim or fly. Think about it.[2]

➤ 2d Consider the trunk of an elephant. Without his trunk the elephant could not survive. His incredible trunk has over 20,000 individual muscles, giving the trunk tremendous versatility. The elephant can pull up a tree, pick up an attacking tiger and smash it to the ground. Yet, with amazing gentleness, the elephant's trunk can pick up a single peanut. What good would a partially developed trunk be to an elephant? The theory of evolution tells us that it had to take millions of years for the trunk of an elephant to fully develop.[3]

There are so many more good examples of why evolution is just a fairy tale, but for simplicity sake and time we will stop with these. For more research on your own, check out these websites:

1. Access Research Network-www.arn.org
2. American Scientific Affiliation-asa.calvin.edu
3. Institute for Creation Research-www.icr.org
4. Reasons to Believe-reason.org
5. DissentFromDarwin.org

Charles Darwin, the founder of evolution, said that the "cell" was simple. The cell is anything but simple. The cell is complex. For review of the complicated cell see earlier section under "The Cell."

Evolution claims we all began in a primordial ooze, and that species over billions of years adapted to life and the species that formed.

The fossil record does show evidence of microevolution (which is one kind of fish or species evolves into another of the same species), but there is no evidence for macroevolution (one species evolves into a different species).

Darwin admitted that millions of 'missing links,' transitional life forms, would have to be discovered in the fossil record to prove the accuracy of his theory that all species had gradually evolved by chance mutation into new species. Unfortunately for his theory, despite hundreds of millions of dollars spent on searching for fossils worldwide for more than a century, the scientists have failed to locate a single missing link out of the millions that must exist if their theory of evolution is to be vindicated."[4] There should be an abundance of transitional fossils, in fact millions since it has been estimated that over a billion species have existed in earth's history. For 150 years paleontologists have been busy digging, classifying, and looking for these transitional fossils in a worldwide hunt. Billions of fossils representing about 250,000 species have been scrutinized.[5] Wouldn't you agree that Darwin's predicted missing links should have been found by now?

"Scientists concede that their most cherished theories are based on embarrassingly few fossil fragments and that huge gaps exist in the fossil record." Time magazine, Nov. 7, 1977.

Kent Hovind has a standing offer reward of $250,000 to anyone who can give scientific proof for evolution. He has offered this at numerous universities and it is posted on his website at www.drdino.com. Evolution lacks normal intelligence. Nothing gets better by itself. Things deteriorate with time and age.

BOTTOM LINE:
1. THE MISSING LINK IS STILL – MISSING!
2. AFTER ALL THESE YEARS, APES STILL PRODUCE APES, DOGS STILL PRODUCE DOGS-- NOT CATS, GIRAFFS ARE STILL GIRAFFS, FISH ARE STILL FISH, BIRDS ARE STILL BIRDS, HUMANS PRODUCE HUMANS AND WE ALL LIVE TOGETHER ON THIS EARTH AT THE SAME TIME. There are no transitional fossils.

As stated so well by Dr. Henry Morris, "In the real world, tales about fishes and frogs turning into men are found only

in books of fables and fairy tales; they have no proper place in books purporting to be textbooks of science. When a beast is transformed into a man in a moment, it is called magic; when the beast becomes a man over a million years it is called evolution. The factor of time becomes the fairy's magic wand! It seems that for a person to believe in evolution he must practice what the Bible states, "And they shall turn away their ears from the truth, and be turned to fables." 2 Timothy 4:4"[6]

Problem is- refusing to know the truth, won't make deception truth. If we choose evolution with all its exposed frauds and inconsistencies, then we have no hope for anything better when our short time here on earth is done and therefore, no real purpose for living.

Let's look at the facts here:

The Big Blast theory says that a big blast exploded from nothing and that chaos created everything. The evolution theory actually has two different ideas but basically says again nothing created something and that man evolved from apes originating from a green slime. As we have pointed out, neither one of these makes sense. We would

roll our eyes at the suggestion that a 747 jet ₂g. just appeared in our empty garage by an explosion. Why would logical people believe this incredible continuing universe, planet, and human life got here spontaneously? Did the 911 explosion create chaos and disorder or complex life and needs?

There must be an intelligent Creator to have created the intricate details on this planet. To believe that something as complex as the human eye or body could have just happened out of chaos or coincidence or adaptation would

be like believing that a tornado ₂h. could hit a junkyard and create a Boeing 747. What about a car? If you kept your garage empty long enough would a car eventually evolve there? Or as biochemist Michael Behe says, "Which part of a mousetrap can be removed and still leave you with a functioning mousetrap?" The answer is that nothing can be removed without completely disabling the mechanism. It was first conceived by a mind, then created by an intelligent agent. Even a mousetrap, a simple component, has to be created and made." If you came upon Mt. Rushmore, would you think the wind formed the heads of our presidents? Airplanes, cars, cell phones, computers and other complex things as well as non-complex items can

always be traced to a designer. 2i.

The Big Bang Theory

According to the Big Bang theory the universe formed from an extremely dense hot state and continues to expand. The phrase "Big Bang" was actually coined as a joke by Fred Hoyle who didn't believe in the Big Bang theory, but even though it was just a joke, it stuck. The Big Bang theory says that a tremendous explosion started everything. Imagine a blast making an incredibly complex, organized world. Can you think of any explosion that has produced order? Does a terrorist bomb create harmony? Big bangs cause chaos. Try this experiment: Empty your garage of every piece of metal, wood, paint etc. Make sure there is nothing there. Nothing. Then wait for ten years and see if a Mercedes evolves. Try it, if it doesn't appear, leave it for 20 years. If that doesn't work, try if for 10,000 years or even 250 millions years. As Jim Holt states, "The universe suddenly exploded into being...The big bang bears an uncanny resemblance to the Genesis command." (Jim Holt, science writer, Wall Street Journal)

The question must be asked, "What made the big bang? How did the big bang explosion create all the beautiful creations we see in nature from the delicate rose to the gigantic Redwood forests? Or how did an explosion create a tiny butterfly, a giraffe, or a miraculous baby from a tiny seed? How did an explosion create life that reproduces more complex life, gravity, continually mixed atmosphere, suspension of the earth, etc? There is no explanation given regarding how that blast got here, nor how it turned chaos into beauty.

Astronomer E. Hubble, founder of Hubble's Law, observed stars are rapidly moving away from each other, the Red Shift Theory. Many scientists are now concluding that the universe, planets and stars began in one place and expanded out, showing that originally all matter; the universe, planets, stars, everything began **in a moment of time** with an explosion that thrust the universe into existence. Many scientists are now saying the universe was the beginning of time and space. <u>The originator of the universe therefore, is outside of time and space.</u>

The Bible says in Genesis 1:1, "In the beginning, God created the heavens and the earth."

You may say, "Yeah, but I can't believe in a superpower, super intelligence or a God I can't see. That is a fair statement. Let's examine that thought a little deeper.

Part B. I Can't Believe in a God that I Can't See

Credit: NASA, ESA, and L. Frattare (STScI)

We have a hard time understanding what we cannot or do not see, and in the case of God, many say they can't believe in a God they cannot see, or another realm such as Heaven and Hell, the angels, demons, eternity, time without end, space or the heavens that go on and on limitless, so vast not even the astronomers know how big space is, it is beyond our comprehension. It is easier to accept the unseen realm of eternity, God, the angels, demons and life after death when we realize all the things we don't see but we rely on such as:

➢ The vast expanse of the heavens, the stars, other galaxies that we never knew were even out there until recent years and even now, barely have a clue.
➢ Gravity. We can't see gravity, but it holds the earth in place and holds us on the earth. Much of the galaxy is invisible dark matter, particles that we can't see. Many scientists are now saying that as much as 90 percent of matter could be dark matter.
➢ The atmosphere. Air. We don't see it, but we have to have it to survive.
➢ DNA- We are made up of atoms that we cannot see

without an electron microscope. We have billions of cells smaller than the dot on this page and the DNA in those cells determine things such as eye color, hair color, gender, etc. We can't see our DNA, but it is part of us and even scientists tell us they don't understand it.

➢ Speed of the earth - We can't see or feel how fast we are moving, but as we read, we are speeding along without knowing it at tremendous speeds.

➢ We can't see our emotions, but we sure feel them. We can't see the human soul but we know it exists and that it is part of every human on earth, yet it has no physical property and no scientific instruments can even detect its existence.

➢ We can't see the wind, but we see what it does.

➢ There are many things we see in our own perception, but that perception can be wrong oftentimes. Such as, the moon appears to give off light, but the moon has no light, it only reflects the light from the sun.

There are many, many things we can't see and we don't understand, but that doesn't mean they don't exist. Though we can't see them, there is evidence that they exist. The same is true of God. As we have begun to see, there are evidences of a Supreme Creator, and this Creator has shown evidences in His nature, in the heavens and in His letter, the Bible to us.

As Ray Comfort has so well stated, *"The question of who made God can be answered by simply looking at space and asking, 'Does space have an end?"' Obviously, it doesn't. If there is a brick wall with 'The End' written on it, the question arises, "What is behind the brick wall?" Strain the mind though it may, we have to believe (have faith) that space has no beginning and no end. The same applies with God. He has no beginning and no end. He is eternal. The Bible also informs us that time is a dimension that God created, into which man was subjected. It even tells us that one day time will no longer exist. That will be called "eternity." God Himself dwells outside of the dimension He created (2 Timothy 1:9, Titus 1:2) He dwells in eternity and is not subject to time. Because we live in the dimension of time, logic and reason demand that everything must have a beginning and an end. We can understand the concept of God's eternal nature the same way we understand the concept of space having no beginning and no end-by faith. We simply have to believe they are so, even though such thoughts put a strain on our distinctly insufficient cerebrum."* [7]

If it can be shown that the Bible is the Word of God, then a host of other objections can be answered by simply referring to Scripture itself.

When a document is proven to be true, then we are foolish to ignore it. So far, we have seen several facts that make the Bible worth considering, so let's continue on and see what history, geography, and prophecy tells us in researching answers to our four questions.

Digging for Truth from the Past

Chapter 3

Historical and Archaeological Evidences

Beit Shean Roman Theatre escavations, Israel (Lloyd)

Questions: Can we learn more about history from facts given in the Bible through archaeological research? Does history prove or disprove the Bible? Can the people and places be documented outside the Bible? Do archeological findings agree with or contradict the Bible?

Fact: The historic people and geographic places referenced in the Bible have been subjected to the most concentrated examination ever given to any book.

Not one single discrepancy has ever been found in these books which would lead one to doubt that they were written by the men to whom they are attributed.

Archaeological evidence time and again has confirmed the accuracy of these books (we will be looking at a quick overview of archeological evidences shortly.)

The Bible has been scrutinized but found to be 100% accurate!

Part A – Geographical Historical Evidence

As Henry M. Morris points out in his book, *Many Infallible Proofs*, "The 19th century higher critics, for example, used to deny the historicity of the Hittites, the Horites, the Edomites and various other peoples, nations, and cities mentioned in the Bible because other ancient historians had not mentioned them. This argument, however, has long since been defeated by archaeologist's digs and finds.

The same is true of historical information regarding kings and empires. The conquest of Canaan by Joshua, the destruction of Jericho, the historical information of the kings of Israel and Judah, the Babylonian conquest and the return of the Jewish people from exile, are all now considered to be historical, whereas until the last century they were denied!"[1]

It is significant to note that the names of forty different kings of various countries, mentioned at various times in the Old Testament have been found, always consistently with the times and places associated with them in the Bible.

Nothing at all exists in ancient literature which has been even remotely as well confirmed in accuracy as has the Bible. Even those names which once were doubted by the critics, (Belshazzar, Darius, etc) have now long since been confirmed.[2] There are hundreds of Biblical cities that have been verified in archaeological digs. You can look them up via the internet @ www.carm.org. as well as other places.

There are many historical places and events which could be cited for historical evidence of the Bible, but for the sake of time and space, I will only list three here and you may research more on your own.

1. Since critics have discounted the Bible on its claims regarding the city and civilization of "the Hittities," who are mentioned in eight different chapters in the Old Testament, we'll begin with this so called "myth" of the biblical critics. They said there was no such place or people as the Hittites. Was there such a place?

Dr. D. James Kennedy writes, "When Dr. Hugo Winckler went to the area to dig where the Hittities were supposed to have lived, he discovered over forty of their cities, including their capital, along with a great number of monuments describing their activities. Commenting on a treaty between the Hittites and the Egyptians that the Bible describes, one English critic said there was no more chance for a treaty to have existed between the Egyptians and the Hittites than between England and the Choctaws. Yet, spelled out on a plain wall in one of the uncovered cities of Egypt was found the whole treaty between Egypt and the Hittites! Numerous Babylon inscriptions have now proved the Hittites to have been a great super-power located between Egypt and Babylonia, so large that all of Egypt and Babylonia were considered to have been tribes of the Hittites. <u>Yes, the Hittites have been found ... just where the Bible said they were.</u> Their extensive empire has been substantiated, their conquests discovered, and the names of their kings wrestled from the long dark tunnel of history."[3]

2. Another historical find in the Biblical story most of us have watched on television is, "The Ten Commandments" where the Bible tells us that the Pharoah oppressed the Israelites and caused them to build for him the store cities of Pithom and Raamses. We remember the story of how they first built with mortar and straw. Then they had to gather their own straw, and finally they had to build the bricks without any straw at all. When Sir Flinders Petrie later discovered the sites of Pithom and Raamses, he noted some incredible things about them. They were built with mortar—something found nowhere else in Egypt. Moreover, the lower layers were built of brick in which was stubble instead of straw. In the second and upper layers were bricks made without straw.[4]

3. Since most of us are familiar with the story of Jericho and the walls falling down we'll look at this historical site. The Bible says that Joshua fought the battle of Jericho, but the critics said that it never happened. One does not just walk around a city and have walls fall down flat. But what did Professor Garstang, British archaeologist and authority on Hittite civilization, discover when he came to the site of Jericho to dig? He states: "As for the main fact, there remains no doubt the walls fell outward so completely that the attackers would be able to clamor up and over their ruins into the city." Why is that so unusual? Because walls do not fall outward. Ordinarily they fall inward, but in this

case the walls were made by some superior power to fall outward, as the Bible says. The critics also declared that the account is obviously factitious because it says the Israelites marched around the city seven times in one day. You could not walk around a modern city of one hundred thousand people seven times in one day, and Jericho was described as a great city. But Garstang's investigation provided an interesting fact about Jericho; it was smaller than the sites upon which many large metropolitan churches are built. Having been to Jericho many times, I know that I could walk around it seven times in one morning and play a set of tennis before lunch! Again the critics were proven wrong.[5]

Over 25,000 sites have been discovered that pertain to the Bible. A hundred years ago many of the cities, empires, people and events contained in the Old Testament books were unknown to modern day historians and

archaeologists. [3a] Many scholars seriously doubted the historical accuracy of the Bible for this reason. They could find no independent verification for the Hittites, for example, which are very prominently mentioned in Genesis, Numbers and Joshua.[6]

An army of learned men and women have dug, sieved, sifted, translated, photographed, and picked many of the obvious sites apart in the land of the Old Testament.

Thousands upon thousands of individual pieces of evidence have been compiled. Lost cities have been found, empires rediscovered. The finds have corroborated the scriptural accounts, and the places mentioned in the Bible have been located just where the Old Testament books said they were.⁷ This is in stark contrast with how archaeology has proved to be devastating for Mormonism. Although Joseph Smith, the founder of the Mormon church, claimed that his Book of Mormon is "the most correct of any book upon the earth," archaeology has repeatedly failed to substantiate its claims about events that supposedly occurred long ago in the Americas. Lee Strobel, former legal editor of the Chicago Tribune, writes, "I remember

writing to the Smithsonian 3b. Institute to inquire about whether there was any evidence supporting the claims of Mormonism, only to be told in unequivocal terms that its archaeologists see "no direct connection between the archaeology of the New World and the subject matter of the book." As authors John Ankerberg and John Weldon concluded in a book on the topic, "In other words, no Book of Mormon cities have ever been located, no person, place, nation, or name has ever been found, no Book of Mormon artifacts, no Book of Mormon scriptures, or inscriptions ...nothing which demonstrates the Book of Mormon is anything other than myth or invention has ever been found." However, the story is totally different for the Bible!⁸

Today you may visit the uncovered walls of the old city of Jericho, the excavated stables of Solomon at Megiddo, the ruins of Shusham, city of Queen Esther, drink from Jacob's well, etc. etc. Piece by piece, like a gigantic jigsaw puzzle, the Old Testament history is being unearthed.⁹

Part B. Historical Evidences of the Man Jesus of Nazareth

Since our search is for the truth of how we got here, why we are here, what is our purpose, and where we will go after we die, then in researching Biblical evidence it must show 100% accuracy. Because the relevancy of Jesus Christ in the Bible is the central theme, we must research to see if the man Jesus Christ ever existed, and if he lines up with the claims he makes about himself in the Bible. So, we'll continue our investigation on the man Jesus Christ of the Bible.

"Christianity is the only religion in the world that is based upon historic evidences. The evidence for Jesus Christ is absolutely overwhelming! No one can disbelieve in Christ because of a lack of evidence.[10] What evidence is there to prove Jesus Christ really existed?

Proving a historical person's existence

How do you prove that a person in history actually lived without birth certificates or official documents? How do we know Alexander the Great or Julius Caesar or Cleopatra really lived? One way is that people wrote about them. Another way is by the marks and monuments they left on the course of history. Did Jesus Christ really exist according to history?

Historical documents outside of the Bible

[3c.] Writings confirming Jesus of Nazareth's birth, ministry, death and resurrection include many non-Christian writers of that era. I will name just four with limited detail and you can look them up for more detail if you want.

1. Josephus, a Jewish historian (AD 37-100) wrote a lengthy article in Antiquities, book 18, chapter 3. "Now there was about this time Jesus, a wise man, if it be lawful to call him a man; for he was a doer of wonderful works, and taught men…and he was followed by many Jews and many Greeks.

2. Roman historian Tacitus (AD 55-117) who mentions Jesus and Christianity in a passage recording Nero's burning of Rome (an historical fact) and that Jesus had suffered under Pilate.

3. Pliny, governor of Bithynia in Asia Minor (from 109 to 111) wrote to the Emperor Trajan explaining, among other things, how he handled the Christians and their honor of Christ.

4. Lucian of Samosata – (Second Century Greek satirist) who wrote about the Christians still worshiping the man who was crucified in Palestine and their eternal beliefs even to the point of being tortured to death.

The following <u>facts</u> about Jesus were written by early non-Christian sources:

- Jesus was from Nazareth.
- Jesus lived a wise and virtuous life.
- Jesus was crucified in Palestine under Pontius Pilate during the reign of Tiberius Caesar at Passover time, being considered the Jewish king.
- Jesus was believed by his disciples to have died and risen from the dead three days later.
- Jesus' enemies acknowledged that he performed unusual feats they called "sorcery."

- Jesus' small band of disciples multiplied rapidly, spreading as far as Rome.
- Jesus' disciples lived moral lives, and worshipped Christ as God."

Hostile Witnesses-Non Christians

Some of the best evidence comes from what a lawyer terms 'hostile witnesses!' [..]d. His enemies, such as those who sought to have him crucified and had the most to gain by denying Jesus' existence. These sources are not sympathetic to Jesus and any evidence given by hostile witnesses carries extra weight. Jews are not sympathetic witnesses to Jesus. They do, however admit that a man named Jesus lived during the time claimed by the New Testament writers, and that He preached in the synagogues during His ministry. He is regarded by them as a rabbi who held heretical views. Moslems also claim that a man named Jesus lived. Many secular writers of Jesus' time also wrote about him.

And last and most important are those who were closest to Jesus, the disciples. The first four gospels in the New Testament of the Bible go into detailed account of this man, Jesus. (We'll research the validity of the gospel writers in the next chapter.) They all are specific on his birthplace, his character, his occupation, places he went, things he did, claims he made. The 27 New Testament books claim to be written by authors who knew Jesus or received firsthand knowledge of him from others, as well as hundreds of witnesses living at the time of these writings who had perfect opportunity and desire to deny the things written about this man if they were not true, but no one, including hostile witnesses denied the facts and testimonies written about him.

Yale historian, Jaroslav Pelikan stated, "Regardless of what anyone may personally think or believe about him, Jesus of Nazareth has been the dominant figure in the history of Western culture for almost twenty centuries...It is from his birth that most of the human race dates its calendars, it is by his name that millions curse and in his name that millions pray."

I will not give a detailed listing of archaeological confirmations of Scripture because it would be too lengthy, but I will list some good books for the interested reader in Appendix 1. <u>It can be stated that Biblical history has been so thoroughly examined and corroborated by archaeological digs and research that informed scholars no longer question it.</u>

Historical Geography

The geography of the case for the historical Jesus is easily verified and straightforward. Jerusalem, Bethlehem, and Nazareth all exist today, and Nazareth hasn't changed all that much in two thousand years. Jerusalem tour guides will show you many archaeological sites and artifacts dated from the first century which bear the name of Jesus Christ.

<u>Compared to Other Historical People</u>

But even more convincing is the argument that just as Julius Caesar, Alexander the Great, and Darius changed the course of history and have indisputable monuments to their lives, Jesus left the church which bears His name and has had a powerful effect on the course of history.

The very fact that we reckon our calendars to B.C. and A.D. divisions testify that a man named Jesus lived. (Definitions for B.C. and A.D. are—Before Christ and Anno Domini-In the year of our Lord Jesus Christ.) There is more real evidence, consisting of hard, verifiable facts, which document the historical Jesus than there is evidence for most characters in history, such as Marc Antony, Cleopatra, Helen of Troy, and others who are accepted by historians the world over.[14]

More books have been written about Jesus than about any other person in history. Numerous institutions and organizations have been founded in his name, including schools, hospitals, and humanitarian works. Universities such as Harvard, Yale, Princeton, and Oxford are but a few universities that have Christians to thank for their beginning. Among people of every nation are former drug and alcohol dependents, prostitutes, and others seeking purpose in life who claim Jesus to be the explanation for their changed lives.

If Jesus didn't exist, one must wonder how a myth could continue to be so prevalent throughout history.

The facts show Jesus of Nazareth did in fact exist, but before we explore what is so extraordinary about this man, let's first examine the credibility of the Bible. How can we trust it, and what evidence is there to show that it is reliable and inspired by more than mere man to give us the answers we are looking for regarding life and death and everything in between? What makes any book reliable for testing its contents?

Testing Ancient Books

Chapter 4

Reliability of the Scriptures

Image:Beinecke-gutenburg-bible.jpg
Wikimedia Commons 4a.

The Bible is the number one best seller of all time and the biggest seller every year, selling approximately 44 million copies every year. The Bible has been translated in over 1700 languages. Compare that to Shakespeare which has been translated into 60 languages. The Bible is the most studied, most read and is published in more languages than any other book. It has been more scrutinized and tested than any other book.

THE SCHOLARS TEST FOR RELIABILITY

The following list is the way scholars test for factual evidences on any ancient writing--let's see how the Bible stacks up using those tests.

1. Details of names, places, events corresponding with other sources.
2. Number of copies of the original documents in existence.
3. How large of a time gap is there between the original writings and the earliest copies?
4. How well does a document compare with other ancient history?

Test #1 – Names, Places and Events Corresponding with other sources.

Archaeology agrees with the Bible regarding geography, historical people, and historical events over and over again, and though it is the most scrutinized book, no contradiction has been found – in fact, quite the opposite-everything in all the above areas have been confirmed! Archaeologists have found exactly what the Bible said regarding historical geography, kings, people, events in every case researched.

We see that the first test has been met so let's move on to the 2nd, 3rd, and 4th tests of validity. Tests #2, 3, and 4 will be analyzed together.

New Testament reliability excels above other Manuscripts

The New Testament is constantly under attack and its reliability and accuracy are often contested by critics. But if the critics want to disregard the New Testament, then they must also disregard other ancient writings by Plato, Aristotle, and Homer. This is because the New Testament documents are better preserved and more numerous than any other ancient writing.[1]

Let's look at what has been accepted by historians as valid for other books of the same general period. Read the following two comparisons brought out by Robert Faid in "A Scientific Approach to Christianity.

> ➢ Caesar's Gallic War, written about 50 B.C. is based on only ten good copies, the earliest copy of which dates from about 900 A.D. Historians do not dispute the validity of this book although almost a thousand years separate the original from the oldest surviving copy.
> ➢ The History of Thucydides is taken from only eight copies which date from over 1300 years after the original was written. Historians do not question the authenticity of this book.

Of course, neither of these books makes the claims made by the books of the New Testament, but we are considering only the validity of authorship and translation and the reliability of the test. In comparison with only ten manuscripts dating 1000 years after the original for the Gallic War; and only eight copies of History of Thucydides, 1300 years after the writing of the original, the New Testament manuscripts available for study number in the thousands, with many of them going back to the life of most of the writers.[2]

Refer to the following chart to see time gaps and time spans of ancient writings compared to the Bible.

The Bible, Fact or Fiction?

Author[3]	Date Written	Earliest Copy	Approx. Time Span between original & copy	# of copies
Caesar	100-44 B.C.	900 A.D.	1000	10
Plato	427-347 B.C.	900 A.D.	1200 yrs	7
Pliny	61-113 A.D.	850 A.D.	750 yrs	7
Herodotus	480-425 B.C.	900 A.D.	1300 yrs	8
Thucydides	460-400 B.C.	900 A.D.	1300 yrs	8
Aristophanes	450-385 B.C.	900 A.D.	1200	10
Catullus	54 B.C.	1550 A.D.	1600	3
Tacitus	100 A.D.	1100 A.D.	1000 yrs	20
Aristotle	384-322 B.C.	1100 A.D.	1400	49
Sophocles	496-406 B.C.	1000 A.D.	1400 yrs	193
Homer (Iliad)	900 B.C.	400 B.C.	500 yrs	643
New Testament	1st Cent. A.D. (40-100 A.D.)	2nd Cent. A.D. 125 A.D.	less than 100 years	24,000

3

As you can see, there are thousands more New Testament manuscripts than any other ancient writing. Most Biblical scholars agree that the New Testament documents were all written before the close of the first century which means that if Jesus was crucified in 30 A.D. as historically recorded, the entire New Testament was completed within 70 years of Jesus' crucifixion. *This is important because it means there were plenty of people around when the New Testament documents were written who could have contested the writings.*

In other words, those who wrote the documents knew that if they were inaccurate, plenty of people would have pointed it out. But we have absolutely no ancient documents contemporary with the first century that contest the New Testament texts. Even critical scholar John A.T. Robinson has admitted, "The wealth of manuscripts and above all the narrow interval of time between the writing and the earliest extant copies, make it by far the best attested text of any ancient writing in the world." [4]

Carbon 14 Dating

The discovery of the Dead Sea Scrolls at Qumran in 1947 had significant effects in corroborating evidence for the Scriptures. The ancient texts, found hidden in pots in Qumran caves confirm the reliability of the Old Testament text.

The manuscripts date from the third century B.C. to the first century A.D. and give the earliest time window found so far. The Qumran texts have become an important witness for the divine origin of the Bible, providing further evidence against criticism.

Carbon 14 dating, used in combination with other scientific tests such as handwriting analysis and/or pottery finds is a reliable form of scientific dating when applied to material several thousand years old. Both the writings and the pottery containing the ancient writings, along with handwriting analysis and textual analysis date the manuscripts before 100 - 300 B.C. (at least 100 years before the birth of Christ.) There is no doubt that the Qumran manuscripts of the Bible came from the century before Christ and the first century A.D. Archeologists use a combination of different methods to date artifacts, including Carbon 14 dating along with other items and documents found at the same locations or containing data at the same time period.

This is important when looking at prophecy predictions to determine fulfillment of past prophecy so we can trust prophecies and predictions regarding our future and what lies ahead for us.

The Bible Stands Alone—It is Unique

➤ The Bible is unique in its circulation. The printing press was invented in 1450 making it possible to print books in large quantities. The first book printed was the Bible. From that day forward the Bible has been read by more people and printed more than any other book in history! Over one billion Bibles had been distributed by Bible societies around the world by 1930. By 1977 Bible societies alone were printing over 200 million Bibles each year. This would indicate that it is worth checking out. The Bible continues to be the #1 seller every year.

➤ The Bible has been translated into over 1,700 languages. No other book even comes close.

➤ As you can see from the previous chart, there are several thousand more Biblical copies than any other historical ancient writings and most scholars agree they were written during the lifetimes of anyone who would dispute their accuracy and yet none are found.

➤ Under the inspiration of God's Holy Spirit, the authors wrote on hundreds of controversial subjects with complete harmony from the beginning to the end. There is one unfolding story, one central theme: the redemption of mankind through the Messiah, Jesus Christ. Jesus left heaven to come to earth and dwell with man, so that man can go to heaven and dwell with God forever.

The Bible was written over a period of 1500 years, by 40 plus authors with different vocational backgrounds ranging from fishermen, shepherds, kings, a doctor, tax collector, generals, historians, from three different continents (Africa, Asia and Europe), three languages, written on hundreds of subjects and yet when they are brought together they are all in complete harmony. As Josh McDowell writes, *"Lest anyone think this isn't something marvelous, try this challenge. Find ten people from your local area having similar backgrounds, who speak the same language...then separate them and ask them to write their opinion on only one controversial subject, such as the meaning of life. When they have finished, compare the conclusions of these the writers. Do they agree with each other? Of course not. But the Bible did not consist of merely ten authors, but forty. It was not written in one generation, but over 1500 years...and yet the Bible is a unity."* [6]

➢ No other book has been so attacked throughout history as the Bible. Only the Bible has withstood 2000 years of intense attack by critics and prospered. In A.D. 300 the Roman emperor Diocletian ordered every Bible burned because he thought that by destroying the Scriptures he could destroy Christianity. Anyone caught with a Bible would be executed. But just 25 years later, the Roman emperor Constantine ordered that 50 perfect copies of the Bible be made at government expense. The French philosopher Voltaire, a skeptic who destroyed the faith of many people, boasted that within 100 years of his death, the Bible would disappear from the face of the earth. Voltaire died in 1728, but the Bible lives on. History shows that 50 years after Voltaire's death, the Geneva Bible Society moved into his former house and used his printing presses to print thousands of Bibles.

➤ The Bible is unique in the fact that it contains 100% accuracy of fulfilled prophecy. No other book, religion, or secular writer has ever made the astounding claims and meticulous, specific, detailed prophecies that the Bible has, or better yet had them come to 100% fulfillment of every prophecy given except the Bible alone. This is both astounding and miraculous. Some people such as Jeanne Dixon, and Nostradamus have made some general predictions which have had very little accuracy, and remember without 100% accuracy you cannot trust their validity.

➤ Only the Bible contains detailed prophecies about the Savior of the world. Jesus made astounding claims about Himself. No other religious leaders made such astounding claims and yet Jesus not only made them, He fulfilled them with traceable writings and documents.

How to Recognize a True Prophet

Chapter 5

Prophetical Evidences
Past, Present, Future

It is important to take the time to talk about the differences between prophecy and fortune tellers because in our search for facts on how to know why we are here, what is our purpose and where we are going, we must know who or what holds the answers to these questions. Anyone or anything that can accurately predict the future with 100 percent accuracy has credibility in considering what it teaches. Prophecy is very important because in any facet, it is a miracle that is testable. All we have to do is see if the events come to pass in order to verify or reject a prophet, religion, or psychic.

Part A. Prophets verses Psychics – What's the Difference?

To consider whether modern psychic's accuracy compares with biblical prophets, let's take Jean Dixon as a case study. This American psychic seemed to have a special ability to foretell events. But upon analysis her reputation seems unwarranted. For instance, during the three presidential elections held in 1952, 1956, and 1960 Dixon prophesied who the candidate would be for each of the major parties in all three of those elections, as well as who would win each election. Want to know how well she did? She missed all three of the candidates, all of the parties, and all of the winners of all the elections. Another prediction Dixon had was a vision that on February 5, 1962, a child was born in the Middle East who would transform the world by the year 2000. This special man would create a one-world religion and bring lasting world peace. She saw a cross growing above this man until it covered the whole earth. According to Dixon, this child would be a descendant of the ancient Egyptian Queen Nefertiti.[1] So, where is this guy? Have you seen him? And what about that lasting world peace?

An exhaustive search of her prediction yields two indisputable facts. Her rate of accuracy is equivalent to those guessing the future, and her most publicized fulfillments were prophecies so intentionally vague as any number of events could have been hailed as fulfillments. And take a look at one of Nostradamus's predictions, "Takes the goddess of the Moon, for his Day & Movement; A frantic wanderer and witness of Gods Law, in awakening the worlds great regions to Gods will (Ones Will)." What is that?

This is generally the track record of psychics. When "The People's Almanac" researched the predictions of 25 top psychics, **92 percent of the predictions had proved wrong.** The other 8 percent were questionable and could be explained by chance or general knowledge of circumstances. This certainly explains why psychics aren't winning the lottery.[2]

The difference between prophets and psychics has to do with prophets revealing God's plan for man and psychics marketing 5a. their services for monetary gain.

According to the Hebrew requirements that a prophecy must have a 100 percent rate of accuracy, the true Messiah of Israel must fulfill them all or he is not the Messiah.

In the world of religion, prophecy serves an important function. It becomes one sure way to know if someone is speaking from God or if he is not, for only an omniscient God could completely know and tell (document) the future. They are unique because they do not exist anywhere else. The prophecies in Scripture are specific and detailed. They must be exactly fulfilled. The prophecies cannot possibly be just good guesses because they concerned themselves with things that had no likelihood of ever coming to pass.[3]

Biblical Prophecies

Over 2000 specific prophecies have already been fulfilled dealing with numerous events, the rise and fall of kingdoms, cities, kings, etc. prophesied in the Old Testament and anyone with a good encyclopedia can verify the accuracy of their fulfillments. Though we don't have time to go over 2000 prophecies we'll look at a couple you can easily confirm on the internet. For instance, there are over 100 specific prophecies concerning Babylon's fate.

The Great City of Babylon

Babylon was considered the greatest city in ancient times. The walls were 187 feet thick at the base and enclosed an area of 196 square miles. The city of Babylon was considered impregnable. Babylon was the largest city in the world from 1770 to 1670 B.C. and again between 612 and 320 B.C. It had a population of 200,000. In Jeremiah 51:58, 62 and other places in the Bible, God said that because of the evil in this city it would become desolate. The Great Wall of China is not nearly as large or as strong, though it is older, it still stands today. The walls of Babylon were destroyed and you can check out the history of Babylon on the internet, or at www.wikipedia.com (an encyclopedia)

The Historical Rise and Fall of Four Major Kingdoms
Another major historical era is the prophecy given by God to Daniel through dreams. (Daniel 2) The book of Daniel in the Old Testament gives incredible prophecy regarding the rise and fall of four Empires.

5b.

1.The Babylon Empire 2.The Medo-Persian Empire 3.The Grecian Empire and 4.The Roman Empire. These date from 626 B.C. to 476 A.D. These prophecies were specific, detailed and in order predicting their rise and fall 200-300 years before the events and every one of these incredible prophecies came to pass just as the Biblical accounts foretold. Read the book of Daniel and if you remember or review history you'll remember that those events came to pass just as the Bible predicted. (Refer to chapter 4 for Carbon 14 dating and a list of how archaeologists test for ancient writings.)

For simplicity sake and time we will not expound on fulfilled prophecies of kingdoms, events, places, except to encourage you to refer to Old Testament Bible reading and research on prophecy via the internet or check out books listed in Appendix 1. We will continue our prophecy evidence on the central theme and person of the Bible-Jesus Christ, Son of God, Messiah, Savior to the world.

In all the writings of Buddha, Confucius, and Lao-tse, you will not find a single example of predicted prophecy, whereas the Bible contains 25% prophecy with 100% accuracy! In the Koran (the writings of Muhammad) there is one instance of a specific prophecy, a self-fulfilling prophecy, that he, Muhammad himself, would return to Mecca. Quite different from the prophecy of Jesus who said that He would return from the grave. One is easily fulfilled, and the other is impossible to any human being.[4]

In the Old Testament, which was written hundreds of years before Jesus' birth (proven by scientific dating) there are 61 specific prophecies and 300 references about the Messiah. Let the reader understand here that people in the New Testament asked Jesus if he was the Messiah (Our Savior), not what a Messiah was. They knew what the Messiah was because there were so many prophecies in the Old Testament regarding the Messiah who would come to rescue Israel. So we see the importance of these prophecies being fulfilled because then we find confirmation for the claim of the Bible that it is the Word of God. If such a person has fulfilled the prophecies, then we must listen to him and take him seriously. So how many prophecies are we talking about? How many would it take for you to seriously trust a psychic or prophet? There are over 300 prophecies regarding the requirements for the Messiah. Did anyone fulfill those?

First let's look at just 2 of the specific prophecies about the Messiah in the Old Testament written hundreds of years before his birth.

1. "But you, Bethlehem Ephrathah, though you are little among the thousands of Judah, yet out of you shall come forth to Me the One to be Ruler in Israel, whose goings forth are from of old, from everlasting."(Micah 5:2, NKJ)

2. "Therefore the Lord Himself will give you a sign: Behold, the virgin shall conceive and bear a Son, and shall call His name Immanuel." (Isaiah 7:14, NKJ)

Before considering the other 59 prophecies, stop and think for a moment about how many people throughout history could possibly qualify to be the Messiah that were born of a virgin in the town of Bethlehem.

For those who question the whole virgin birth miracle, in understanding the uniqueness of who the Messiah was and what He came to do as our Savior from a sinful world demands a unique birth as only the Son of God could do and would need to do to redeem sinful man to a holy God. As quoted by Dr. Manford Gutzke, "The virgin birth is not a big problem at all for God. If there is a God who created the universe, if He flung the galaxies out from His fingertips, if He painted the night sky with a scintillating Milky Way, then surely for Him to take a tiny seed and place it in the womb of a woman is nothing at all. Why should it be thought impossible that God should simply place a "Y" chromosome in the womb of a woman to produce a child?"

When we consider how incredible every detail of living, breathing, existing in this vast detailed universe is, why would it be difficult to believe God could supernaturally and with purpose send the Messiah to earth in a miraculous way and why wouldn't He?

So we see that the Messiah must come from Bethlehem and be born of a virgin. Impossible by the world's standards.

WHAT ARE THE ODDS?

What are the odds of one person fulfilling just eight of the specific prophecies? In his book *Science Speaks*, Professor of mathematics, Peter Stoner gave 600 students a math

probability problem 5c that would determine the odds for one person fulfilling eight specific prophecies such as the Messiah would be betrayed by a friend for 30 pieces of silver. The students calculated that the odds against one person fulfilling all eight prophecies are astronomical – one in 100,000,000,000,000,000,0000. (Verified by the American Scientific Association to be thoroughly sound) To illustrate that number, Stoner gave the following example, "First, blanket the entire Earth land mass with silver dollars 120 feet high. Second, specially mark one of those dollars and randomly bury it. Third, ask a person to travel the Earth and select the marked dollar, while blindfolded, from the trillions of other dollars."5

Let's look at six more of Professor Stoner's predictions for a total of 8 including the dates they were predicted/prophesied, along with the dates they were actually fulfilled.

1. **The Messiah would be from the line of King David**
   Jeremiah 23:5 (600 B.C)
   Fulfilled – Luke 3:23, 31(4 B.C.)

2. **A messenger would be sent to proclaim the Messiah.**
   Malachi 3:1(500 B.C.)
   Fulfilled – John 1:26(27 A.D.)
3. **The Messiah would appear riding on a donkey.**
   Zechariah 9:9(500 B.C.)
   Fulfilled – Matthew 21:7(30. A.D.)
4 . **People would cast lots for the Messiah's clothing.**
   Psalm 22:18 (1000 B.C.)
   Fulfilled – John 19:23-24 (30 A.D.)
5. **The Messiah would have his hands and feet pierced.**
   Psalm 22:16 (1000 B.C.) **(Crucifixion** – This was prophesied
   long before crucifixion was invented as a form of capital punishment
   by the Persians and a thousand years before it was made common
   by the Romans.)
   Fulfilled - Luke 23:33 (30 A.D.)
6 . **The Messiah would be betrayed for 30 pieces of silver.**
   Zech. 11:13 (487 B.C.)
   Fulfilled – Matthew 26:15 (30 A.D.)

Some have objected to the fulfillments saying that Jesus fulfilled the Messianic prophecies by living in such a way as to intentionally fulfill them. Hmmm, let's think about this. How could anyone have control over his lineage, ancestry, specifically how he would die, how much a friend would betray him for and why would anyone in their right mind try to manipulate these details to their own death and detriment?

Part B. Evidences of Jesus' Resurrection

Since the beginning of time, men and women have wondered what happens to their loved ones, as well as themselves after we die? It is an age old question. So, in answering our fourth question, "Is this all there is?" or "Where will I go after I die?" we must first look where we have found the best answers and evidence thus far. This is obviously a crucial question since it encompasses a space of forever.

In chapter 3 we have seen convincing evidence that the

man Jesus of Nazareth really did live and that many prophecies were fulfilled regarding his life.

Jesus made claims that, if true, have profound implications on our lives. According to Jesus, you and I are special, part of a grand cosmic scheme.

Other moral and religious leaders have left an impact—but nothing like that unknown carpenter from Nazareth. What was it about Jesus Christ that made the difference? Was he merely a great man, or something more? Jesus never claimed to be a great religious leader. Jesus claimed to be God, Creator of the Universe, the only way to Heaven.

Jesus claimed to be the Messiah, who came from Heaven. Jesus also claimed to be equal to God; and the Savior of the world who would die for the forgiveness of sin and would rise from the dead three days later. Jesus performed many miracles and signs that supported his claims. (In other words, he didn't just talk, he backed up his claims with actions.) Every miracle was done in public, not secret. Jesus fulfilled more than 100 prophecies in the Old Testament. There is evidence of each one of these prophecies being fulfilled, and no one during the writings of these fulfillments contested them in any historical writing. They have been documented as fact in secular, non-Christian writings, as well as other religious writings as having fulfilled the original prophecies predicted hundreds of years before Jesus' birth.

Jesus, himself, predicted that he would suffer, die, and rise again. He told his disciples months before his crucifixion that he must be killed and after three days would rise again. (Mark 8:31)

The tombs of Muhammad, Buddha and Confucius are

occupied, but the tomb of Jesus Christ is empty to this day. Why is that significant? It is through the power of the resurrection that Christ is declared the Son of God and it is by the resurrection that His atoning sacrifice for our sins is declared to be accepted by God in order to make a way for us to join him in Heaven. This is the center of the Christian faith. With it everything stands or falls. Therefore all skeptics through nineteen centuries have aimed their largest guns at the resurrection of Jesus Christ.[6]

If the evidence shows validity that Jesus truly did rise from the dead, together with the other facts we have already seen regarding the Bible's amazing claims, then it is should be studied as sound testimony. It is unique when compared to all other religions, theories, philosophies, and should be held up as worth our time to read in seeking answers to the most important questions of life regarding our purpose in this life and what happens to us after we die.

First note that the evidence for the resurrection of Jesus Christ has been examined more carefully than the evidence for any other fact of history! D. James Kennedy points out in his book, *Why I Believe*, the fact that "the resurrection

has been weighed [5d.] and considered by the greatest of scholars, among them Simon Greenleaf, the Royal professor of law at Harvard from 1833 to 1844 who helped bring Harvard Law School to preeminence and who has been called the greatest authority on legal evidences in the history of the world. When Greenleaf turned his mind upon the resurrection of Christ and focused upon it with the light of all the laws of evidence, he concluded that the resurrection of Christ was a reality, that it was a historical event, and that anyone who examined the evidence for it honestly would be convinced this was the case.[7] The same is true with Frank Morison, a British lawyer who set out to write a book repudiating the resurrection of Jesus Christ. He wrote his book, but it was not the book he set out to write. As he examined the evidence for the resurrection of Christ, this skeptical lawyer found it so overwhelming he was forced to accept it and become a believer. The book he did write, titled Who Moved the Stone, sets forth the evidence for the resurrection of Christ and its first chapter is called, "The Book That Refused to Be Written." Lew Wallace also set out to write a book disproving the deity of Christ and His resurrection and ended up writing a famous book defending it. That book was titled Ben Hur. The evidence for the resurrection of Christ, for those who take the time to examine it, is very significant."[8]

What's the Story? What is the Resurrection?

5e.

This is obviously a hard concept to believe – that someone could die and 3 days later rise again, so let's put ourselves in the role of a skeptic who needs compelling evidence before we can believe such an incredible event really occurred. In the book, *Who was the Real Jesus?*, Chapman, James and Stanford explain the absurdity of false proclamation in such an easily revealed event of that day. The article is entitled, "*Self Prophecy*." I will include it here to better explain the events. "In advance of his death, Jesus told his disciples that he would be betrayed, arrested and crucified and that he would come back to life three days later. That's a grand plan! What was behind it? Jesus was no entertainer willing to perform for others on demand; instead, he promised that his death and resurrection would prove to people (if their minds and hearts were open) that he was indeed the Messiah. Bible scholar Wilbur Smith remarked about Jesus, when He said that He himself would rise again from the dead the third day after He was crucified, He said something that only a fool would dare say, if He expected longer the devotion of any disciples-unless he was sure He was going to rise. **No founder of any world religion known to men ever dared say a thing like that.** In other words, since Jesus had clearly told his disciples that he would rise again after his death, failure to keep that promise would expose him as a fraud. ''[9] True? You bet.

As prophesied hundreds of years earlier, as well as by Jesus shortly before his death, Jesus was betrayed by a friend for 30 pieces of silver, convicted of claiming to be God and condemned to die by crucifixion on a wooden cross. If you watched the Passion of Christ or read the Bible, you know He was brutally beaten with a Roman cat-o-nine-tails, a whip with bits of bone and metal that rips flesh. He was punched repeatedly, kicked and spit upon before being nailed through his hands (wrists) and feet to

the cross. [5f.] Pilate wanted confirmation that Jesus was dead before allowing his crucified body to be buried. So a Roman guard thrust a spear into Jesus' side. The mixture of blood and water that flowed was a clear indication that Jesus was dead. Upon taking him down from the cross he was buried in Joseph of Arimathea's tomb. In accordance with Jewish burial customs, Jesus would have been wrapped in a linen cloth with about 100 pounds of aromatic spices, mixed together to form a gummy substance and applied to the wrapping of cloth about the body. After the body was placed in a solid rock tomb, an extremely large stone weighing approximately two tons was rolled by means of levers against the entrance of the tomb. Roman guards (a unit of 4-12 trained Roman guards) sealed the tomb with the Roman seal and secured it with around-the-clock guards. (Roman guards had to guard their prisoners with their own lives, because if the seal was broken this meant automatic crucifixion upside down to the guards.)

While all this was taking place, Jesus' disciples were in hiding out of fear for their lives.

THIS SHOULD HAVE BEEN THE END OF THE STORY BUT SOMETHING MORE HAPPENED.

The news 5g. should have read, "Jesus, the proclaimed Messiah Dead!" As we all know, the Jesus movement didn't end there. So, what happened? What happened to make Christianity today the world's largest religion?

Evidences for the Resurrection
Fact 1. An empty tomb and no body to be found anywhere.

Jesus was buried in Joseph of Arimathea's tomb. Joseph belonged to a member of the Sanhedrin. In Israel, at that time, to be on the council was to be extremely important.

Everyone knew who was on the council.
Joseph must have been a real person, as no one disputed
him in any writings, secular or religious at the time and the
Jewish leaders would have exposed the story as a fraud in
their attempt to disprove the resurrection. Also, Joseph's
tomb would have been at a well-known location and easily
identifiable. If Jesus' body was anywhere to be found, his
enemies would have quickly exposed the fraud. Tom
Anderson, former president of the California Trial
Lawyer's Association, summarizes the strength of this
argument:

*"With an event so well publicized, don't you think that
it's reasonable that one historian, one eye witness, one
antagonist would record for all time that he had seen
Christ's body? The silence of history is deafening when it
comes to the testimony against the resurrection."*[10]

As Josh McDowell writes in his booklet, *Christianity,
Hoax or History,* "The disciples of Jesus did not flee to
Athens or Rome to preach that Christ was raised from the
dead. Rather, they went right back to Jerusalem, where, if
their claims were false, the falsity would be evident. The
empty tomb was 'too notorious to be denied.' This was not
done in a corner. The burial site was well known not only
to Christians and Jews but also to the Romans. This is why
Dr. Paul Atlthaus states that the Resurrection 'could not
have been maintained in Jerusalem for a single day, for a
single hour, if the emptiness of the tomb had not been
established as a fact for all concerned.' Both Jewish and
Roman sources and traditions admit an empty tomb. And
no shred of evidence has been discovered in literary

sources, epigraphy, or archaeology that would disprove this statement."

So we have an empty tomb and no body---

What happened that caused the followers of Jesus to stop mourning after only 3 days, stop hiding and all of a sudden go from being fearful cowards to boldly claiming that they had seen Jesus alive?[11]

Fact 2. Jesus appears to His disciples & five hundred witnesses.

Every eyewitness account reports that Jesus suddenly appeared bodily to his followers. All the disciples saw Jesus on more than 10 different occasions. They wrote that he showed them his hands and feet and told them to touch him. He later appeared to more than 500 followers on one occasion. Legal scholar John Warwick Montgomery stated, "In 56 A.D. Paul the apostle wrote that over 500 people had seen the risen Jesus and that most of them were still alive. (I Corinthians 15:6) It would be impossible to believe that the early Christians could have made this all up, preached it among those who would have easily produced the body if they could have."

Fact 3. Jesus' followers turn from cowards to bold witnesses for Christ.

A fact of history that has stumped historians, psychologists, and skeptics alike is that these eleven former cowards were suddenly willing to suffer humiliation, torture, and death. All but one of Jesus' disciples were slain as martyrs. Would they have done so much for a lie, if they had really not seen Jesus alive and the tomb empty? As written in the book, *Who Was the Real Jesus,* "The Islamic terrorists on September 11 proved that some will die for a false cause they believe in, but no one will be tortured and die for something they know to be a lie or make up such as the resurrection. They had to have seen a resurrected Jesus. But even if they all conspired to lie about Jesus' resurrection, how could they have kept the conspiracy going for decades without at least one of them selling out for money or position?" Moreland wrote, "Those who lie for personal gain do not stick together very long, especially when hardship decreases the benefits."

Chuck Colson, implicated in the Watergate scandal, pointed out the difficulty of several people maintaining a lie for an extended period of time. He said, "I know the resurrection is a fact, and Watergate proved it to me. How? Because twelve men testified they had seen Jesus raised from the dead, then they proclaimed that truth for 40 years, never once denying it. Every one was beaten, tortured, stoned and put in prison. They would not have endured that if it weren't true. Watergate embroiled twelve of the most powerful men in the world-and they couldn't keep a lie for three weeks. You're telling me twelve apostles could keep a lie for 40 years? Absolutely impossible "[12]

People today will hardly cross the street for something they believe. The disciples had nothing to gain by fabricating a lie, no ulterior motive, but in fact they had everything to loose. They all gave up everything and faced a life of hardship with no earthly reward. They suffered greatly to passionately tell everyone what they had witnessed all the way to their deaths. It should be noted that these disciples came from all walks of life from a tax collector, a doctor, to fisherman, etc. who were so transformed by the **POWER** of the resurrection (life after death) that they literally gave their lives to tell everyone about what they had witnessed in Jesus as the Messiah and the resurrected Son of God. Instead of Christianity dying at the cross, it grew.

Fact #4 – Easter 5i.

Do you know when the holiday of the first Easter began? History traces it all the way back to the city of Jerusalem in A.D. 30 after Jesus' death and resurrection. When the Christians celebrated Easter the greeting was: "Christ is risen!" and the response: "Christ is risen indeed!" Many people do not make the connection between the church and the resurrection, but all scholars have.

Fact #5 - Christian Art.

In the catacombs of Rome, from the time of the persecutions, we find carved into the walls representations of the resurrection of Christ as a part of the very earliest beliefs of the Christians. And Christian hymns were sung to the resurrected Jesus Christ.[13]

Fact #6 - The Christian Church is the largest institution that exists or has ever existed in the world.

It is known by all historians and is an indisputable fact of history, not faith, that the largest institution in the history of the world began in A.D. 30 in Jerusalem when the apostles began to preach that Jesus Christ rose from the dead. The very heart and substance of the message of the early Christians was that Christ was risen from the dead. The first message delivered at Pentecost was entirely about the resurrection of Christ. All sources, from unbelievers, to hostile witnesses as well as Scripture declare that the church was spread everywhere because of this teaching that Christ had risen from the dead. It is a fact.[14]

Fact #7 - The Silence of Jesus' Accusers

The silence of Jesus' accusers and hostile witnesses as well as anyone in that era disputing anything regarding Jesus' character, miracles, death, resurrection is further evidence. No-one disputes these facts. If these events hadn't happened, we would see evidence, but quite the opposite is true. Even non-Biblical historians have recorded these events. To name just a few you can read the writings of

Josephus (Antiquities, XXXIII.iii.) 5j. in the first century, who mentions Jesus' crucifixion, Pliny the Younger (Pliny the Younger, Epistles, X.96) and The Talmud, (Babylonian Talmud, Sanhedrin 43a), dating from the second century AD, mention the crucifixion of Jesus. Even Pontius Pilate, procurator of Judea who condemned Christ to death, wrote of those extraordinary activities to Tiberius Caesar in an apparently well-know account that has been referred to by several other historic personages.[15] Included in the account, Pilate told of the events and his order to crucify Him even going into depth on how the sun grew dark for 3 hours in the middle of the day. (The Bible gives detail regarding the sky being dark from the sixth hour to the ninth hour-middle of the day while Jesus hung on the cross.)

Fact # 8 - Detailed Prophecy of the Resurrection

No religious leader, psychic, or secular leader has ever made the claims that Jesus did! Seriously think about it. Against all odds, all explanation, there is detailed evidence to support the resurrection giving credibility to Jesus' claims that stand up with complete accuracy that Jesus fulfills all prophecies regarding being the Messiah and having power over death. No other explanation can be given to account for all this except that the Bible is supernatural in origin. That should prompt us to seriously consider finding out what the Bible has to say.

Past   Present   Future   Prophecy

The Bible gives us the details of past prophecies, future to them but history to us, as well as present prophecy that we see being fulfilled right before our eyes as well as future prophecy.

Want to know what the future holds for planet earth, for America, Europe, the Middle East?

Well, just like God through Daniel predicted the four world kingdoms that would rise and fall hundreds of years before the events, and by checking history we can see that each kingdom rose and fell just as God foretold in the Bible; just as the Bible prophesied in detail the Messiah's coming and just as Jesus told of the events of His death and resurrection before they happened, so God also tells us in the Bible what is about to happen next! God gives specifics in incredible supernatural detail to the events currently taking place and those soon to happen in all their force. In light of how much is at stake, one would be wise to pay attention to prophecy. **These historical prophesied events are not fiction, they are fact!** God predicted these major events which are known to the world, and we would be foolish to ignore fulfilled prophecy of the past as we would be foolish to neglect to study current events in prophecy because our (your) entire future is at stake.

The World as we Know it is About to Change

"I am God and there is no other; I am God, and there is none like Me, declaring the end from the beginning, and from ancient times things that are not yet done."
Isaiah 46:9-10

Chapter 6

Current Events–Living in the 21st Century

Our Future Revealed!
One Final Kingdom

6a.

Fulfilled Prophecies Leading to the Return of Christ

(Easy to Read Spreadsheet stating Eleven Signs Predicting Christ's Return following this chapter.)

People have been saying for years that Jesus' return is very near, but the reality is that the Bible tells us what must happen first before Jesus returns and the events that must happen preceding Jesus' return <u>did not occur until after 1948</u> and later. For hundreds and even thousands of years things remained relatively the same in the realm of travel, knowledge, wars, technology, medicine and predictions. Prophecies that made no sense to our grandparents and even our own parents are now not only understandable, but are taking place right before our eyes. Most people do not know what the government and major corporations currently have set in place soon to be imposed on the public! I will tell you some of these and alert you to websites with information that will astound you.

What was written in the Bible thousands of years ago, looked like science fiction to our grandparents and even some of our parents, but as you read this and easily research these facts for yourselves, you will see, that what our previous generation could not fathom is on the horizon and now being set up to take place momentarily. We see more prophecy fulfilled in one month than our grandparents did in their entire lives!

Everything you will read here, you can look up for yourselves. The information was given in the Bible written 2000-5000 years ago. The fulfilled prophecies, many hidden from you, can be found on the internet, in various magazines such as Time, Endtime Prophecy, etc. and all you have to do is look. People have asked, "When will Jesus come back and what is the sign of the end?" Jesus tells us what the signs are in several places in the Bible, including Matthew 24 and Mark 13, Ezekiel 36-39, and Revelation. Throughout the ages, some of these signs have taken place, but it wasn't until 1948 when Israel became a nation 6b. that the culmination of all the signs could all come together. In Luke 21:28-29 (NKJV), Jesus says, "Now when these things begin to happen, look up and lift up your heads, because your redemption draws near."

Matthew 24:32-34 (NKJV), "Now learn this parable from the fig tree (represents the nation of Israel): When its branch has already become tender and puts forth leaves, you know that summer is near. So you also, when you **see all these things**, know that it is near-at the doors! Assuredly, I say to you, this generation will by no means pass away till all these things take place." It is when you see **all these things** take place, not just a few. What "things" you may ask. Check these out. See attached spreadsheet for simplified detail and references.

1. MANY WILL BE DECEIVED

According to the Bible, false teachers will lead millions away from God's truth. Make it a priority to study your Bible so that you will know God's Word and no one will be able to deceive you.

2. ISRAEL MUST BECOME A NATION.

This was fulfilled May 14, 1948.

3. REGATHERING OF THE JEWS TO ISRAEL.

Jews are currently re-gathering from other countries by record numbers. Israel is God's prophetic time clock. Watch Israel for end time events. Tiny Israel is in the news daily while large countries are not. Think about it. Many countries are now going against tiny little Israel, but they will not completely take over Israel, because God will not allow it.

4. KNOWLEDGE EXPLOSION

The Bible says in the last days knowledge will increase. Knowledge stayed pretty much the same for over 2000 years, now look at technology in the different areas:

A. Travel.

For thousands of years people traveled only by horse

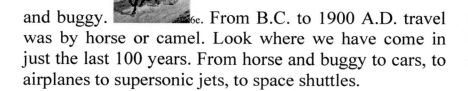

and buggy. From B.C. to 1900 A.D. travel was by horse or camel. Look where we have come in just the last 100 years. From horse and buggy to cars, to airplanes to supersonic jets, to space shuttles.

B. Medical. Speaks for itself. Until the 1900's medicine remained relatively the same. Now we can keep people breathing who can't breathe for themselves, we can transplant organs, replace limbs, cure diseases.

C. Communication.

Again for thousands of years we only had telegraph and telephone. In the last 10 years we have gone from cell phone to mobile phones, sky phones, phones with cameras, faxes, internet, email and internet voice mail.

D. Computers.

In 1973, a computer housed at College of the Redwoods took a whole room to house. Now almost every home has at least one computer and they are small enough that you can carry them around with you. You can't keep up with technology. Computers, cameras, and cell phones are almost out-dated as soon as you get them. Knowledge is doubling every 6 months, (remember in the previous generations, nothing changed for hundreds of years. **We are the generation living in the age of technology.**

5. Rampant sex, violence, immorality.

Yes, there has always been violence, but not the way we see it now. Daily we see new reports of mothers murdering their own children, of mass killings in our schools. Nothing is sacred anymore regarding morality or ethics and we are bombarded with it constantly. (See spreadsheet.)

6. Increase in earthquakes, natural disasters, famine, disease.

Though we have always had earthquakes, hurricanes, tsunamis, and disease we have never had them in such high proportions and epidemics as we do now.

7. Satellite TV

The whole world can watch live events at the same time. The significance of this sign in the Bible prophecy is that it foretold that in the last days everyone would be able to see events all over the world at the same time. This could not happen in our grandparent's day as satellite television only came about in the last few years.

8. Nuclear weapons 6f.

Nightly we are made aware of nuclear tension everywhere and have almost grown apathetic and disbelieving regarding it, but it is at our door. Iran is currently threatening nuclear warfare as well as known sources (FBI) reporting they have sleeper cells in 7 major US cities prepared to set off bombs simultaneously. See spreadsheet for this specific prophecy.

9. Wars & rumors of wars.

Nation against nation. Look around you. Terrorist threats, nuclear threats everywhere from several countries. Iran boastfully threatens to wipe both Israel and America off the map. Countries everywhere are attaining nuclear capability that could wipe out all civilization-unlike the wars of the past.

Russia has never been friends with Iran, but currently, after 2500 years, Putin and Ahmadinejad have become buddy-buddy and are aligning military strength. Furthermore, Putin has gone to several Islamic and middle-eastern countries to build military alliances with them. Keep in mind they hate Israel and remember Ahmadineajad's threats. He fully intends to carry them out. This coming war is unlike any other. Why? Because the strict Muslims believe that their Mahdi, (12th Imam) will not come until the world is in chaos. They think they can usher him in faster by creating chaos. They think they are rewarded by killing Jews and Christians. They believe their own suicide to kill infidels will bring themselves and their families eternal rewards. That is why we cannot negotiate with them.

For anyone truly interested in how close we are to the most catastrophic war ever, read Ezekiel 38 and 39 in the Bible and you will see what the Bible forecasts for World War III and the end to this world as we know it. Just as the book of Daniel forecasted the consecutive rise and fall of four world empires, the book of Ezekiel tells us what is going to happen in this catastrophic war. This is not fiction. History shows the complete fulfillment of past prophecy, we would be wise to pay attention!

10. CASHLESS SOCIETY – The Bible says that a day is coming when no one would be able to buy or sell without a mark on their right hand or forehead. (see Revelation 13:16)

For thousands of years this prophecy was impossible—now for the first time in history we are able to buy and sell without cash. In America we are 97% cash free. The predicted "Cashless Society" is being instituted. People are currently taking advantage of buying and selling by the wave of their hand under a laser light in numerous places just for convenience. This lights the way for instituting the Mark of the Beast. Microchip implants are currently taking place and the only thing that prevents commerce and banking networks from using the chips and implants on everyone is public fear. It is ready currently, it is in place and it is only a matter of time before it is enforced. **People all over the world as well as in the United States already have a chip implanted under their skin with all their personal data.** In 2007 in Palm Beach, Florida, 200 Alzheimer's patients have been implanted with the VeriChip. Digital Angel, also in Palm Beach, Florida is producing microchips by the tens of thousands.

This is serious stuff! Read the Bible and watch the news remembering that the Bible foretold these events thousands of years ago. This is a significant event in knowing how close the Mark of the Beast is and therefore the return of Christ.

Look at how much currency has changed in the last few years: 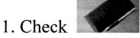 6g. For hundreds of years only gold or cash was exchanged. It went from cash to:

1. Check
2. Debit cards & Credit cards
3. Electronic Transfers
4. Smart Cards
5. Cards that give rewards to use their card
6. Microchips-Animals and people being implanted with microchips just as the Bible foretold!

Wikimedia: RFID
human implant-6h.

We never have to deal with cash anymore!

Systems currently in process that most people don't know about: (References following)

1. Microchips now required on all registered animals and many humans are now being implanted with these chips. Among several people already implanted with chips, 200 Alzheimer patients living in Florida now have a Verichip implant under their skin.
2. RFID – Radio Frequency Identification – Already used by Walmart, Proctor & Gamble, now in passports, some credit cards and numerous other places.
3. Spychips
4. Verichip
5. Real ID *(Advertised as National Id but actually Global Id.)*
6. EPC – Electronic Product Code soon to replace UPC code.
7. Digital Angel – Tracking Device. See "World Net Daily" 8/13/2000.

Be advised: As this book is being written in 2009, by the time you read this information implants and technology will far exceed the numbers and data given. You will hear these terms on TV and radio. Pay attention and be prepared. Do a study of your own. Listen for terms describing a One-World Monetary System, as well as a One-World Government and One-World Religion.

11. One-World Government

Over 2500 years ago the Bible prophesied about a One-World leader who would rule the world. There will be a

One-World Government, One-World Dictator, One-World Financial System and One-World Religion. This is just about to happen!

Currently our world leaders all over the globe are discussing plans on how to incorporate this global system. We have a global financial crisis. The Euro currency has been promoted for years and now with the American financial crisis and the collapse of the US dollar, China and Russia as well as numerous other countries are pushing the One-World Financial system and One-World Government. In July 2009, at the G-8 summit held in Italy, Russian President Medvedev introduced a world sample test coin. He held up a coin with the words, "United Future World Currency" surrounding five different types of trees leaves sprouting from a single stem, apparently representing groups of nations. On the reverse side of the coin was a large "1" and the words, "Unity in Diversity" along with the words, "Test-limited issue, 2009,"

The world today is looking for someone to take charge of the spiraling financial, political, terrorist catastrophes and most nations are jumping on the global bandwagon and looking for a One-World Leader.

The Bible clearly tells us this will happen and tells us when it will happen. This One-World leader will be the "Antichrist" (a charismatic, intellectual, charming persuasive deceiver, who promises world peace when there is no peace.) The man will come on the scene shortly before Jesus returns to earth for the final time. Don't you find it amazing, that a book written hundreds of years ago, before computers and the possibility of incorporating a sophisticated One-World financial bank and system, prophesied this would happen? **Watch the news, it is**

being planned now and it is just about to take place.

References to outline above and spreadsheet following chapter:

Holy Bible

Internet – look up words such as:

Microchip Implant or Human Microchip

Caspian

Verichip

Spychips

RFID

Digital Angel

Mark of the Beast

666

Big Brother

Real ID

(Type in anything pertaining to the cashless society. You will be amazed!)

1. Endtime Magazine – 1-800-endtime or www.endtime.com
2. Spychips by K. Albrecht & Liz McIntyre (Found in Government & Political section in Borders)
3. Time magazine/search topics
4. Wikipedia/search topics
5. Worldnetdaily.com
6. David Jeremiah, "What in the World is Going On?" www.turningpointonline.org
7. Jack Van Impe ministries

ALL THESE THINGS ARE TAKING PLACE. ALL YOU HAVE TO DO IS GET ON THE INTERNET AND CHECK FOR YOURSELVES!

Pretending these things are not out there, won't change the fact that they are. The Bible predicted (prophesied) Jesus would come the first time and told several events to precede His coming and events of His life, death, and resurrection. We have seen the evidence showing the validity of the Bible's claims. If a book proves to be accurate and prophetical, a person would be foolish to ignore it, especially when the consequences are so great. The Bible also predicts (prophesies) Jesus' second coming and the events immediately preceding His final return before the end of this world as we know it! Be prepared and knowledgeable and then you will have nothing to fear, because all these things were prophesied in the Bible. God told us these things would take place, and He said to encourage each other, because He is coming soon and has prepared a place for us. For those of us who know Him, we have better things ahead!

Let the reader understand the difference between the two major events soon to take place. They are separate events:

1. First to take place will be an event known as the rapture. This is where true Christians will be changed in a moment, in the twinkling or blink of an eye and will meet the Lord in the air to forever be with the Lord. You will know the rapture has taken place when millions of children and Christians are gone. All the events given that would precede that rapture have taken place. The rapture can happen any time. You can read about this exciting event in the Bible in the books of 1 Corinthians 15:51-52 and 1 Thessalonians 4:16-17.

2. Jesus' second coming. The antichrist (One-world ruler) will come on the scene 3 ½ to 7 years before Jesus Christ

returns the second and final time. For anyone wanting to know what will signal Jesus second return, just notice that the rapture has taken place, a one-world government will be instituted as well as a one-world religion and one-world money system. This will happen quickly and will only last 3 ½ to 7 years. (Remember that the first time Jesus came, he came as a baby, meek and mild, for the sole purpose of one day dying for our sins, making a way for us so that we may join Him in Heaven for all eternity.) The second time Jesus comes, He will **not** come meek and mild, He will come as a lion, purifying and judging the earth. With the second coming of Christ, comes judgment.

Life is soon to change here on earth.

6j.

FAREWELL

At any time those who have accepted Jesus Christ into their hearts may leave this world via the "rapture" explained in the Bible. At any time the Antichrist can come on the scene. At that time there will be 7 horrendous years or less and then the judgment for unbelievers. This is all predicted in the Bible, and predictions in the Bible have a history of coming true. Make sure you are ready to meet Him. His hand is on the door and you will soon be facing your awards ceremony **or** you'll be facing judgment and Hell! There are numerous scriptures promising rewards to those who serve Him and a glorious, exciting future awaits those who know Jesus Christ as Lord. For those of you who don't know if you are going to heaven or hell, let me ask you this question, "If you knew that today would be your last day here on earth, how would you spend it? What would you do with this day? If this were your last day, then tomorrow would be the first day of your eternity-your forever life. Where will you spend eternity? Many people plan for retirement, which lasts only a few short years, but neglect to plan for their eternity. The average life span is 70-80 years, but life doesn't end here on earth, your soul continues on after your body dies. Your body is only like

the glove on a hand, you take off the glove and you

still have the hand. The same is true of the soul. When the human body dies, the soul continues on, your soul never sleeps. We will live forever somewhere. For some it will be in a place that the Bible says is so wonderful that we can't even imagine how awesome it will be, but for others it will be in never-ending hell! Ignore it, laugh at it, don't believe it, but this will happen nonetheless! For some reason, people believe they are doing God the favor by deciding to believe in Him. In reality, it is out of His great love for us that He offers us such a great gift. It doesn't matter whether you believe it or not, just like a caterpillar doesn't know or believe it will be transformed into a butterfly, nonetheless, it changes into a beautiful butterfly. Like a caterpillar (worm) has no idea what lies ahead for him, if we humans would only study and heed the Bible, we would fall on our knees in gratitude and anxiously tell everyone we know what lies ahead to ensure their eternal soul would reside in Heaven. Just as many of us have heard the horror stories of demons on this earth, you can be sure Hell is a reality and demons are real and no one wants to spend eternity with such evil, agony and separation from everything good.

In Chapter 7, we will present the options according to the only proven supernatural book and the best seller of all time– the Bible, but first look at the following spreadsheet to get a quick overview of prophetical events now taking place. Compare what couldn't have happened twenty years ago, i.e. cashless society, to what is transpiring in the world today.

SIGNS OF JESUS CHRIST'S
SECOND COMING

"When you see **all** these things taking place know that Jesus' return is near." Matthew 24:33

Jesus said He would return after all these things were in place, not before. No other generation has experienced all these events nor has any other generation had the technology that we have today. **This is the first generation to meet the criteria to see the Lord's return**!

If you follow this spreadsheet all the way through, it will look like science fiction, except that if you watch the nightly news you will see all these events playing out.

Note to the reader - when reading the following spreadsheet, there are four columns to each page. Two pages make one sheet.

The Bible, Fact or Fiction?

Subject (Signs)	Scripture	Date Fulfilled
1. Many will be deceived.	Matthew 24:4, "Take heed that no one deceives you."	Currently
2. Israel will again become a nation.	Matt. 24:32-34, " Learn this parable from the fig tree: When its branches become tender & puts on leaves, know that it is near-at the doors. **This generation will not pass away till these things take place.**"	1948
3. Re-gathering of the Jews.	Jeremiah 23:7-8, "….as the Lord lives who brought up the descendents of the house of Israel from the north country & from all the countries where I have driven them, and they shall dwell in their own land."	1950 on / 1999
4. Knowledge Explosion / Travel	Daniel 12:4- " ….Many shall run to and fro, and knowledge shall increase."	Currently
Medical	…..knowledge shall increase	
Communication	….knowledge shall increase	
Computer	….knowledge shall increase.	

Fulfillment
Many are being deceived. Study God's Word (the Bible) so that no one deceives you. Millions are following false religions.
The tree represents Israel and it has bloomed. Israel became a nation in 1948. Read the history and miracle of this small group of people regaining their nation. **This is the generation that will see the Lord's return!**
Between 1988 and 1996 more than 750,000Russian Jews returned to Israel and they are continuing to return in record numbers. Russian Jewish immigration alone doubled in the first 2 months of 1999.
For hundreds of years people traveled by horseback. It wasn't until almost the 1900's did the automobile come into our lives. Within a hundred years we went from automobile to aircraft, to the space shuttle to supersonic jets.
Medical science didn't change until the 19th century and now among numerous technological advances that we have made, we are now able to keep unconscious people breathing indefinitely, transplant human organs, etc.
From telegraph to telephone to cell-phone, faxes, sky phone, text msgs and voice mail on your internet, it's nearly impossible to keep up with technology. For hundreds of years we only progressed to telegraph and telephone, but look at where we have come in the last ten years.
This is really a class all by itself regarding the knowledge explosion category. In the 1970's it took a big room to house one computer. Now almost every home has at least one computer. We have computers we carry with us. We can research and communicate with the click of a button. This scripture is definitely being fulfilled in our day.

The Bible, Fact or Fiction?

Subject (Signs)	Scripture	Date Fulfilled
5. Rampant sex, violence & immorality	Romans 1:24-28 "God gave them over in the sinful desires of their hearts, to sexual impurity for the degrading of their bodies with one another…women exchanged unnatural affections and men were inflamed w/lust for one another... Matthew 24:37-39…But as the days of Noah were so will the coming of the Son of Man be….they were eating, drinking & marrying…& did not know…. Matthew 24:12…lawlessness will abound, the love of many will grow cold."	2004
6. Increase of earthquakes, famines & disease	Luke 21:11, "And there will be great earthquakes in various places & famines & pestilences."	2002--now
7. Satellite TV	Revelation 11:3, 7-10 speaking of the two witnesses – "…then those from the peoples, tribe, tongues & nations will see…."	Now possible w/ satellite
8. Nuclear weapons	Zechariah 14:12 "…Their flesh will dissolve while they stand on their feet, their eyes will dissolve in their sockets, and their tongues will dissolve in their mouths."	Currently

Fulfillment

In the 1950's a married couple could not be shown together in the same bed on TV. Now we have complete programs geared around sex, affairs and homosexuality. In 2004 a measure was put on Calif. voter ballets trying to legalize marriage to people of the same sex but it was voted down by the majority of people, only to have a judge over-rule the people and married same sex people. This agenda is going from state to state. It is important to remember that God judged and destroyed Sodom & Gomorrah due to the practice of sodomy-homosexuality. We must realize that we are higher than animals--- we were created in God's image.

We have always had violence, but not at the level we see it now. Mothers are killing not only their unborn babies, but also their young children. Monthly a wife turns up missing. Terrorism is at an all time high and murder is rampant.

We have always had earthquakes, famine, disease, but if you have watched the news in the last two years you have seen unprecedented devastation in climatic proportions from earthquakes, tsunamis, hurricanes, disease, & famine.

Only with the technology of satellite television has it become possible for everyone to watch events as they are happening. Not possible until this generation. An event that happens in the Mideast can be broadcast simultaneously all over the world. This scripture tells of the murder of two witnesses being murdered and the whole world can see it at once. Not possible until satellite.

Remember that this scripture was a mystery to our grandparents & parents generation until the bombing of Hiroshima. Nuclear bombs today are thousands of times more powerful than the bombs dropped on Hiroshima.

The Bible, Fact or Fiction?

Subject (Signs)	Scripture	Date Fulfilled
9. Wars everywhere	Matthew 24:6, "And you shall hear of wars & rumors of wars…nation will rise against nation & kingdom against kingdom…"	Currently
	Ezekiel 38 and 39 - Read amazing prophecy written regarding Russia, Persia (Iran), and several middle-Eastern and Asian nations that will align to come against Israel. The Bible clearly states what is just about to happen in the Middle East.	In the news
10. Cashless Society - Mark of the Beast	Revelation 13:16–17 "He causeth all…, to receive a mark on their right hand or their forehead, and no one may buy or sell except one has the mark or the name of the beast, or the number of his name…his number is 666."	Currently being set up
11. One World Government	One-World Government, One-World Currency, One-World Religion. (Revelation 13:7, 8 "…and authority was given him over every tribe, tongue and nation. ..")	Currently being set up

Fulfillment

Again, we have always had war, but now wars are on every front. Several countries are threatening nuclear war and terrorists are everywhere. The FBI knows they are already here in America just waiting for further instructions. The tiny country of Israel is in the news daily—pay attention to the middle eastern countries and Israel. This is where the last battle (World War III) will be fought. Life as we know it is about to end. Iran is currently threatening to wipe both Israel and America off the map and you can be sure that this evil leader will keep his promise as soon as they are ready. This is more than a political battle with the Muslims. They believe their coming 12th Imam will be hastened by chaos on earth!

Russian's former president, Putin, is aligning with Iran's leader, Ahmidinejad & several other countries who hate Israel. According to Ezekiel chapters 38 and 39, it states that while Israel is thinking all is at peace (because of a negotiated peace treaty) Russia (Rosh) from the North, Persia (Iran) and many other countries will attack Israel from all sides! It will be a war like none other! Know this: God loves Israel and God will defend her. Russia and the other nations will attack, but they will lose. Watch the news as these events unfold and compare what the Bible said would take place in the last days. This is no movie, it is for real!

Until recently, no-one could comprehend this. In our grandparents and parents day a society operating without cash was unthinkable. From cash to check to scanning UPC codes, ATM's, debit cards to electronic transfers and direct deposits, we never have to handle cash. This was predicted in the Bible over 1900 years ago and it wasn't until recently that we have had the technology of buying & selling with a number. This wasn't possible until the invention of computers. Furthermore, microchips are now being implanted in both animals and humans. Beginning in 2008 all animals must be implanted with microchips and over 200 people in the USA have microchip implants. Soon cash will be eliminated.

As we watch the financial crisis deteriorate all over the world, as well as watch the "Global World " Bank popping up on credit cards, and in the media, we can see how this is already transpiring. Listen for anything associated with the title "One-World", EU, United Nations.

Why Are We Here?
Where Will We Go After We Die?

Chapter 7

Choices:
Where Will You Spend Eternity?

According to the signs and predictions in the Bible it won't be long before it is too late to make a choice on where you will spend eternity. Though the events currently taking place show evidence that Jesus Christ is coming soon, even if Jesus waited a little longer before His return so that more people would come to know Him, you could be gone tomorrow in any accident or disaster. Every day 150,000 people pass into eternity. You or a loved one could be one of them. Even if you live out a long life, comparatively it will be very, very short compared to eternity. Being indifferent or indecisive regarding your future will prove to be disastrous for you, because by not choosing to receive Jesus Christ as your Savior and not obeying Him, you reject Him.

You may ask me, "Why do I care where your soul goes? Or what business is it of mine?" The answer is God cares. He loves you and wants you to spend eternity with Him. He has put it in my heart to share with you the truths I have found by doing extensive research and from my personal relationship with Jesus Christ. I will gain nothing whether you choose to believe in God or not, but you will loose everything if you neglect, reject, or ignore the knowledge you have been presented. You see, if I am wrong, I have lost nothing, but if you are wrong, you will loose everything.

Transformed Lives

More prevalent than all the data presented in this book, more than all the facts and evidences supporting an intelligent Creator is the transformation God makes in lives. I can share with you all the facts, but knowing the facts won't get you to Heaven--only knowing Jesus Christ as your personal Savior will get you into Heaven. Because we live in these finite bodies, it is hard for us to comprehend that another realm in the vast expanse really exists. We barely see past our first atmosphere with telescopes and even that realm took us centuries to see. Imagine trying to explain to a caterpillar the problems of flight. It would be impossible to try to explain to it that one

day it will fly upon the flowers and float in the sky.
The caterpillar (worm) can't even jump a millimeter off the ground, and yet God in all His wonder and creativity of making all things new transforms a caterpillar into a beautiful butterfly. God does the same for us when He fills us with His Holy Spirit.

The life of Jesus from His birth to His resurrection was a turning point in the history of mankind. The influence of Jesus has literally changed history.

Probably nothing in human history compares to what has been accomplished by Christian missions. As quoted in

James Kennedy's book, *Why I Believe,* "A writer who returned one hundred and thirty or so years ago from a trip around the world found that missions and missionaries were being bombarded with criticism in the London papers. So he wrote a letter to the paper defending missions; he said the transformation of wild savages in the isles of the South Seas was something to behold, and to make light of this was a heinous crime: 'For a voyager to forget these things is base ineptitude; for should he chance to be at the point of shipwreck on some unknown coast, he will most devoutly pray that the lesson of the missionary may have preceded him.' **The author of that letter to the newspaper was Charles Darwin**. After his return from his around-the-world trip he was transformed. Whether the missionaries had been there or not would probably make the difference between being invited to dinner or being the dinner."

Skeptics have done little to help the brutal natives in the hard-to-reach jungles of some third world countries. Skeptics have built few leprosariums, few hospitals, few orphanages. It has remained for the followers of Jesus Christ to care for the offscouring of mankind.[2]

No matter what the critics say, Jesus Christ of the New Testament changes lives. Millions from all backgrounds, nationalities, races and professions for more than twenty centuries, are witnesses to the sin-breaking power of God's forgiveness through Jesus Christ. E.Y. Mullins writes:

"A redeemed drunkard, with vivid memory of past hopeless struggles and new sense of power through Christ, was replying to the charge that his religion was a delusion. He said: 'Thank God for the delusion; it has put clothes on my children and shoes on their feet and bread in their mouths. It has made a man of me and it has put joy and peace in my home, which had previously been hell. If this is a

delusion, may God send it to the slaves of drink everywhere, for their slavery is an awful reality."[3]

When someone testifies to being addicted for years to drugs, alcohol, pornography or a destructive lifestyle and states that they have been delivered by asking Jesus Christ to come into their heart, then it is only reasonable to believe that if the only difference in their life before and after the change is Jesus Christ as their Lord then it stands to reason there must be supernatural power found in the common denominator of millions of lives who have been changed by Him.

Though I have learned much in researching truth regarding science, astronomy, history and prophecy which reveals exciting truth and evidences of a loving, intelligent Creator; it is the personal relationship I have experienced of a loving God that transformed my life. Although we all face trauma at some point in our life, the way we deal with trauma results in either a destructive or a constructive effect on our life and the lives around us.

While many people become angry and bitter and resort to destructive forms of addictions such as alcohol, drugs, anti-depressants, smoking and other vices just to help them cope with life, others turn to God enabling them to heal and find purpose in helping others.

Some people say that people who need God just need a crutch. I am thankful to be able to say that as a result of having a relationship with Jesus Christ, I don't have to depend on an addiction to get me through the day. Millions of lives have been transformed by the power of Jesus Christ. I am one of them. I have my own story to tell of why I believe in Jesus Christ.

Like many, many people on this earth, selfish decisions

of other people has dealt me some difficult events in my life from my teenage years on up. Because we live in a fallen world, with fallen people we will face difficulties on this earth. This earth is not perfect, as we all know, and until we get to heaven we will have to deal with difficult situations and difficult people. Previous abuse and betrayal directed toward me earlier in my life caused bitterness, anger, self-pity, apprehensions and many tears.

Belief in a personal Savior, has given me peace and strength in the midst of difficulty revealing to me that without a shadow of a doubt there is a personal, loving God who fills my life with joy instead of bitterness, purpose for living and a hope for a better life in my forever future. I have been transformed from a shy, dependent, insecure woman into a woman who now has a passion to help other people experience true freedom, joy, and security found only in Jesus Christ. It is so rewarding and exciting to know that when my life continues after this one, the Bible promises that "No eye has seen, no ear has heard, no mind has conceived what God has prepared for those who love Him." (1 Corinthians 2:9) When I think of all the beauty here on earth and in space, and then read this scripture, I can only surmise-- Heaven must be amazing! Therefore, I can enjoy life here on earth, while looking forward to life in Heaven.

How Can a Loving God, send people to Hell?

God loves you so much, but God didn't make, nor does He want puppets. He won't force you to love Him, because then it ceases to be love. From the very beginning God gave us the power to reject Him. He gives us freedom of choice. But there are only two choices: Heaven or Hell. There is no third choice. You must make the choice before it is too late. People break God's heart every day. One hundred fifty thousand people a day pass into eternity, most without God.

Out of God's great love for people He went through great lengths to make a way for us to spend eternity with Him. But He won't force us to love Him. God sent His only Son to earth to make a way for us to go to Heaven. It is our choice.

Secondly, let me ask you this question using a current day scenario. A man kidnaps a child and assaults the child repeatedly, eventually murdering the child, while the child's parents are frantically, hysterically looking for the child. Several years pass by and the murderer finally gets caught and is sent before the judge. When the man goes before the judge he calmly says to the judge, "Judge, I know you won't send me to prison because you are a good judge, a good man." Would the judge be a good judge if he just let the murderer or rapist go free? Of course not. He should execute justice because he is a good judge. What if the man never got caught and never had to pay for the heinous crimes he had committed? Would God be a good, just God if he just let this man off with no penalty? Would the child's parents and relatives be at peace knowing there would never be any justice? And what about the child? Would God be good, fair, loving if he just let all murderers, rapists, child molesters, thieves, etc. go to Heaven with no consequences?

We live in a fallen world. Two hundred thousand people are murdered every year and one hundred thousand of these murdered victims get no convictions. Should the murderers automatically go to heaven? Do you think God would be a just judge if criminals never paid for their evil against innocent human beings? What then makes it Heaven and what kind of God would He be that loves every human being, even the victim but would let justice fall by the wayside?

God's standards are higher than ours. What should be the standard or the line? God will not tolerate any sin no matter how big or how small. A lie is a lie. There are no little white lies. God says we will even be judged by our words. Where does God draw the line? How many lies are okay, how many items are okay to steal? How many people can we hurt by betrayal? How many times can we disobey God's laws thinking we can get away with it? God says no sin will be in Heaven. Also there will be no tears, no death, no pain, etc. I am so glad that Hitler won't be there and that sin won't be there-- otherwise it would just be another earth all over again. Thankfully, Heaven is where God dwells and Heaven is free of sin. God is Holy and sin separates us from God. Everyone has sinned. The Bible says there is

only One way to heaven   and that is through Jesus Christ. Jesus said, "I am the way, and the truth, and the life; no one comes to the Father, but through Me. (John 14:6 NASB) Jesus also said, "For unless you believe that I am He, you shall die in your sins." (John 8:24 NASB) and "All have sinned and come short of the glory of God." (Romans 3:23 KJV)

To explain this we must go back to the beginning.

Why Am I Here? What is my purpose?
Back to the beginning

An infinite-personal God created the heavens and the earth. (Genesis 1:1) God also created man in His own image. (Genesis 1:26) When God finished creating everything, He said everything was good. (Genesis 1:31). The Bible tells that God walked in the garden with them. He enjoyed fellowship with them.

Man and woman were in the perfect environment that God had created. Everything was provided for them and they only had one restriction-- God told them not to eat the fruit of the tree of the knowledge of good and evil. (Genesis 2:17). The only thing forbidden in this beautiful world they lived in was not to eat the fruit from **one** tree.

Unfortunately, they did eat of the tree (Genesis 3) and the result was broken fellowship with God because they disobeyed Him. Many consequences followed and life on earth has never been the same between God and mankind. Sin came between God and mankind. People have continually rebelled against God. However, because God loves us He promised to restore fellowship with us and make everything right again through the Savior, Jesus Christ, who alone can deliver us from the bondage of sin. (Genesis 3:15)

WE ARE HERE BECAUSE GOD LOVES US AND HE WANTS A RELATIONSHIP WITH US. GOD WANTS US TO SPEND ALL ETERNITY WITH HIM!

The whole spectrum of the Bible shares how God came to earth to dwell among us so that we can go to Heaven to dwell with God for eternity. That is amazing love. The Old Testament repeatedly explained that one day a Savior would come to set us free. And in the New Testament we see that the Messiah, God's Son, our Savior did indeed come as He said He would. You see, no one and nothing, except Jesus, God's perfect Son, can redeem us or make us right with God. If there was any other way to restore our fellowship with God, He would not have had to send His Son to die for our sins. That is why no other religion or religious leader can make things right with God. There is no one perfect except God and His Son, Jesus Christ. No one else can take away our sins. The perfect Son of God shed his blood to redeem us, and bring us back into fellowship with a Holy God. Money, jewels, riches, works could not restore our relationship to God, only the sacrificial shedding of Jesus' blood can restore our relationship.

But Jesus' death on the cross is not the end of the story. Josh McDowell illustrates it this way, "*Suppose a group of us are taking a hike in a very dense forest. As we get deeper into the forest, we become lost. Realizing that we are taking the wrong path now might mean we will lose our lives, we begin to be afraid. However, we soon notice that ahead in the distance where the trail splits, there are two human forms at the fork in the road. Running up to these people, we notice that one has on a park ranger uniform, and he is standing there perfectly healthy and alive, while the other person is lying face down, dead. Now which of these two are we going to ask about the way out? Obviously, the one who is living. When it comes to eternal matters, we are going to ask the one who is alive the way out of the predicament. This is not Muhammad, not Confucius, but Jesus Christ. Jesus is unique. He came back from the dead. This demonstrates that He is the one whom He claimed to be (Romans 1:4), the unique Son of God and the only way by which a person can have a personal relationship with the true and living God."*[4]

God doesn't grade on the curve. His standards are higher than ours. Our sins will keep us out of a righteous Heaven with a non-compromising, intelligent, Holy God. So God had to make a way to cleanse us of sin and restore fellowship with Him once again.

Now, it is quite possible that you think you are good enough to get into heaven because you think you haven't really sinned. Have you kept all the ten commandments according to Exodus 20? Do you know what they are? Let's go through a few of them and see if you have kept them.

> ➤ Have you ever told a lie? There is no such thing as a little white lie. A lie is a lie. What does that make you? A liar.
> ➤ Have you ever taken God's holy name in vain? Anyone who uses God's name as a curse word is

committing blasphemy.
➢ Have you ever stole anything? Even a small item as a child? What does that make you? A thief.
➢ Have you ever committed adultery, slept with a person you are not married to? The Bible says in Matthew, that if a man looks at a woman with lust he has already committed adultery with her in his heart. What does that make you? An adulterer.
➢ Have you kept the Sabbath holy?

That is only 5 of the 10 commandments. On Judgment Day will you be found guilty of any of these? If so, you would end up in Hell. That is not God's will. Romans 3:23 (NASB) says, "For all have sinned and fall short of the glory of God." He provided a way for us to be forgiven. He sent His Son to take our punishment: "God demonstrated His love toward us, in that, while we were yet sinners, Christ died for us."[5] Imagine loving someone so much you would die for them. Imagine the Creator of the universe loving every one of us so much it was worth it to Him, to send His beloved Son to earth to die for our sins and restore fellowship with us.

There is only one way to Heaven and that is through Jesus Christ. John 14:6 (NASB) says, "Jesus said to him, 'I am the way, and the truth and the life; no one comes to the Father but through Me.'" Thankfully, the Bible also tells us that "God so loved the world, that He gave His only begotten Son, that whoever believes in Him should not perish, but have eternal life."(John 3:16) Jesus then rose from the dead and defeated death. God promises everlasting life to all those who confess and forsake their sins, and trust in Jesus Christ. The Bible says in Romans

10:13 (NASB), "Whoever will call upon the name of the Lord will be saved." There is nothing we can do to earn our way into Heaven. It is only by God's love and mercy that we are able to call upon Him to save us.

All you have to do to be sure you spend your eternity in Heaven, is to believe Jesus Christ died for your sins and pray a prayer something like this:

"Lord Jesus, I need You. I am sorry for the wrong things I have done. Thank you for dying on the cross for my sins. Please come into my heart and forgive my sins. Thank you for giving me eternal life. Help me now to live for You. Amen." Your salvation, (way to Heaven), does not depend on emotions or feelings. If you sincerely prayed and asked Jesus to come into your life, He heard you and you are now a child of God. Romans 10:9, "If you confess with your mouth Jesus as Lord, and believe in your heart that God raised Him from the dead, you will be saved."

As a New Christian what do I do now?
➤ Pray everyday. Just talk to God.
➤ Get a Holy Bible and read it everyday. Begin by reading the Gospel of John and then the New Testament.
➤ Turn from your sin and obey God.
➤ Find a Church where they teach from the Bible.
➤ If you have just asked Jesus into your heart, contact a local Bible believing church, or ask the friend who gave you this book to direct you to a good Bible believing church.
➤ Check out the resource section at the back of this book for further resources.

To Sum It All Up

Chapter 8

In A Nutshell

So, why should we believe the Bible is truth, Jesus Christ is our only way to Heaven and God is the Creator of the Universe? Because the Bible is the only book to contain History, Science, Astronomy, Archaeology, and Prophecy. The Bible transforms lives and gives specific answers to where we came from, how we were created, what is our purpose and where we are going after we die. No other book addresses all these areas with answers relevant for all time, past and present.

Answers to Life's Most Important Questions

The exciting news is that there is a source shown to have repeated accuracy and evidences that has been proven over and over again to be trusted. The Bible is a proven book that gives the answers to life's questions that most of us have asked at some time in our life.

1. Where did we come from? God clearly states where we came from and where we are going. In the beginning, **God** created the heavens and the earth ...Genesis 1:1.

2. How and Why did we get Here? God created man in His own image; in the image of God He created him; male and female He created them. Genesis 1:27. God loves people. He created us and He desires fellowship with us. It is hard to imagine that the creator of the universe, who created billions of stars and the great expanse all around us and keeps it all going, wants a relationship with us. But that is why He created us. You are special to God. Isn't that amazing?

3. What is the Purpose of My Life? To enjoy fellowship with God. To love and serve God and others.

4. Where will I go after I Die? That is up to you. The Bible says that it is appointed once unto a man to die and after that to face judgment. (Hebrews 9:27). This is the biggest decision you will ever make. It affects everything you do now and for eternity. Your life will go on forever and it's up to you where and how you spend it. Don't delay such a monumental decision.

NUTSHELL CHAPTER REVIEW

SCIENCE, ASTRONOMY, PHYSICS
Chapter 1 – Planet Earth & the Universe

Part A. Earth is unique in that it is the only known planet to have complex life. That makes you and I special to the Creator who created us. To exist in the cosmos is truly miraculous.

Look at what was written in the Bible before scientists, astronomers and telescopes.

- The earth is round
- The earth is suspended on nothing
- Innumerable stars
- Creation made of invisible elements
- Blood is the source of life

Part B - <u>Our Bodies are truly miraculous</u>.

Humans are specially designed! Make no mistake you are a special creation, loved by your Creator, God.

- The Brain --According to probability scientists, the chance of evolution or even a laboratory of scientists producing a human cell is $10^{119,000}$ to 1, a number we cannot even comprehend. It could never happen. The brain has 12 billion brain cells with 100 trillion connections. The human brain is unique. Humans have both the hardware and software for language above all other breathing things. Humans have the ability to conceptualize-animals don't. Humans have consciences governing our instincts, drives and desires allowing us

to rise to a higher way of life.
- The Eye-The finest camera doesn't even come close to the complexity of the eye. The eye can increase its ability to see in the dark one hundred thousand times. The eye has automatic focus and can distinguish between 7 million colors. The eye must connect to the brain as a keyboard must connect to a computer hard drive.
- The Heart – Beats 100,000 times every 24 hours. Pumps 6,300 gallons of blood a day.
- The Cell- So complicated that scientists say that no one on this earth can explain what makes an individual cell operate!

Evolution & the Big Bang
Chapter 2 – Evolution and the Big Bang

- Evolution says we evolved from lower life forms-from simplicity to complexity, originally from a green ooze, to a rodent, to an ape and eventually to man. Teaches adaptation such as fish turned into birds, and the wings of birds are adaptations from fish fins. The two are completely different. A bird must have light bones (hollow bones) to fly, a fish must have heavier bones to stay under water, and as of yet no transitional fossil has been found between the two.
- For evolution to be true there must be thousands of transitions as evolution requires intermediate forms between species, but there are none! Where there is evidence of microevolution, there is no evidence of macroevolution. If evolution were a fact then the fossil records should shout it to the world, but the truth is they

do not. Though millions of dollars have been spent searching for fossils worldwide, scientists have failed to locate a single missing link that must exist for the theory of evolution to be vindicated.

- The founder of evolution said and believed that the cell was simple, when in truth the cell is incredibly complex. How can you trust the founder of an entire theory being taught to all our children when he was so wrong on something so major?

The Big Bang – States that a big bang created everything. One has to ask, "Where did the Big Bang come from and when have you ever seen chaos create order?" Just as a building needs a builder, a watch needs a maker, so does something as complex as the universe, the earth and people need an intelligent creator. A car doesn't just appear in a garage, a city doesn't just appear in New York, how can we imagine a planet just appears with all the intricacy and detail it had to have to regulate and survive with such precision and beauty and complexity? Think about it.

Part B – Can't See God, How do I know He exists?

Just because we can't see something doesn't mean it doesn't exist. Most of us have never seen outer space, nor another realm, known as the heavens, therefore we have difficulty believing in Heaven and Hell, eternity, space, angels, demons, God, and time with no end. These are beyond our comprehension, but even though we don't see many things, that doesn't mean they don't exist. There are many things we can't see, such as:

- Gravity, but it holds us to the earth and holds earth to its cycle.
- Space--Don't know where it starts nor where it ends, it just goes on and on. Scientists have no idea how big it is. Does it even have an end?
- Atmosphere--Can't see the air we breathe, (unless you live in Los Angeles) and yet the chemicals needed to sustain life are continually being mixed.
- DNA—We can't see it, but DNA determines everything from gender, size, to fragrance to eye color etc.
- The wind--We only see its effects.
- Wrong perceptions such as the moon giving off light. The moon doesn't give off light, it reflects light from the sun.

Historical & Archaeological Evidence
Chapter 3 – Historical & Archaeological Evidences

Part A – Geographical Evidence and Events

- The historic people and geographic places referenced in the Bible have been subjected to the most concentrated examination ever given to any book and not one discrepancy has ever been found. Archaeological evidence time and again has confirmed the accuracy of the Bible. Twenty-five thousand sites have been discovered that pertain to the Bible.

Part B – Evidence of the man Jesus Christ on earth.
The evidence for Jesus Christ living on earth is overwhelming. Check out these facts:

- Several existing secular documents written of Jesus including His birth, ministry, death and resurrection.
- Hostile witnesses wrote facts about Jesus and the miraculous things He did. They did not attest to belief in Him as their Savior but they did attest to the events of His life here on earth.
- Twenty-seven New Testament books were written by authors who personally knew Jesus.
- He was a dominant figure in history. Calendars are dated from His birth. B.C. standing for before Christ and A.D. stands for Anno Domini, translated definition- The Year of Our Lord Jesus Christ.
- Jesus founded the Church which bears His name.
- There is more evidence for Jesus Christ of Nazareth then there is for most people in history such as Marc Antony, Cleopatra, Helen of Troy, Alexander the Great, etc.
- More books have been written about Jesus than any other person in history.
- Former drug and alcohol addicts, prostitutes, and others seeking purpose in life claim Jesus as the explanation for their changed lives.
- Amazingly, Jesus made this worldwide impact as a result of only a three year period of public ministry. That seems nothing less than supernatural.

Reliability of the Scriptures
Chapter 4

- The Bible is the number one best seller of all time every year. The Bible has been translated into over 1700 languages.

- The Bible has been more scrutinized and tested than any other book and yet no discrepancies have been found regarding history, science, prophecy.
- The Bible manuscripts are better preserved and more numerous than any other ancient writing. There are presently 5,686 Greek manuscripts in existence today for the New Testament which far outweighs the others in quantity. Also documented is the amazing difference in the time gap of ancient documents compared to the Biblical documents. Outside the Bible the time gap of these other ancient writings are hundreds of years, whereas the Biblical New Testament time gap is within 100 years. This is important because it shows that people were still alive during the time of the writings and therefore they could have been disputed if they were inaccurate, but there have been no documents that contested these writings.
- Carbon 14 Dating & the Dead Sea Scrolls in 1947 corroborate evidence for the scriptures. The manuscripts found in clay vessels in the caves at Qumran in 1947 date from the third century B.C. to the first century A.D. Carbon 14 dating of the manuscripts, dated pottery and other methods date these to be written at least 100 years before Christ, thereby proving prophecy of Christ.
- Though many in power have tried to destroy the Bible throughout the centuries by burning it, banning it, destroying it, even killing millions of Christians from centuries past and currently in several countries around the globe, the gospel of Jesus Christ, the Bible and Christianity live on and continue to spread.

Prophecy-Past, Present, Future
Chapter 5 – Prophetical Evidences: Past, Present, Future

Prophecy must be 100% accurate to be trusted and used as facts and evidence.

Part A. Prophets verses Psychics

- Psychics have a poor record for accuracy. Psychics inaccurately predict future events for money or fame whereas prophecy must be 100% accurate to be trusted and serves as an important function in that it becomes a sure way to know if someone is speaking from God according to their accuracy. Biblical prophecy is specific, detailed and usually miraculous to accomplish, whereas psychics are usually general in their predictions.

- Over 2,000 specific prophecies have been fulfilled dealing with numerous events such as the rise and fall of kingdoms, cities, kings, etc. and anyone with a good encyclopedia can verify their accuracy. A few good examples are:

- 150 years before King Cyrus was born, he was specifically called by name to be the king that would come into power at a designated time and release the Israelite captives in Babylon to go back and rebuild their temple in Jerusalem.

- Babylon, the largest city in the world at the time, would become desolate because of its evil and as prophesied this impregnable city was destroyed.

- According to Daniel's dreams, four major empires would rise and fall in the succession which was prophesied 200-300 years before the events. The four world kingdoms: Babylon, Medo-Persia, Greece and the Roman empires which all rose and fell just as prophesied.

- No other religion contains specific prophecy with 100% accuracy.
- 61 prophecies of Jesus' birth were analyzed and verified by probability statistics showing that fulfilling just 8 of these would be impossible and yet evidence shows these as facts that came to pass.
- Specific details were given regarding Jesus' death and resurrection. Not only did the Old Testament writers prophecy hundreds of years earlier about how the Messiah would be killed and would rise from the dead, but Jesus, himself, told his disciples of the coming events. The tombs of Muhammad, Buddha, and all other prophets are occupied, but the tomb of Jesus is empty. This is significant, because it shows the power of God to raise His Son from the dead and thereby verifying life after death in another realm-Heaven or Hell.
- Jesus' death was backed up by facts in a populous place by numerous people. Even his enemies wrote things about Him which to this day no one disputes those events. Both secular and Christian writers have documented the events around His death and resurrection proving that Jesus of Nazareth did exist.
- After the resurrection, Jesus appears to the disciples and five hundred other witnesses. The disciples are transformed from cowards the day before His crucifixion to brave witnesses of His resurrection after He arose. The church spread as a result of this miraculous event.
- Easter begins at the first Pentecost and from then on

Easter has been celebrated. The Church began when its founder was raised from the dead. The Church is traced back to the first Easter. (30 A.D.)

Just as past Bible prophecies have come to pass, we can be assured that the prophecies predicted for our generation and the very near future will come to pass. We are blessed to be able to see behind us (history) what laid before them (prophecy), revealing proof that we can trust and know the Bible is the Word of God and what He says will surely come to pass.

Current Events-Living in this Century
Chapter 6 (For References & Detail see spreadsheet)

The major Signs of His Coming – Matthew 24, Ezekiel 37, 38 and Revelation among others.

- Israel becoming a nation – 1948
- Many will be deceived.
- Jews scattered around the world for over 1900 years, would return to Israel in record numbers.
- Knowledge Explosion--Everything remained the same for the over four thousand years until about the 1900's. Since the time of the computer age, knowledge has increased exponentially and now they say that our knowledge is doubling about every six months. Think about it, computers, phones, cameras are out of date almost as soon as you buy them.
- Rampant sex, violence and immorality. Look how things have changed in just the last twenty years.
- Increase of earthquakes, famines, pestilences and

disease.
- Wars everywhere
- Satellite TV
- Nuclear Weapons
- Cashless Society – Rev. 13:16
- World Government, One-World Financial system, One-World Religion. Rev. 13:17, 18
- Severe persecution of Christians

Transformed Lives
Chapter 7 – Where will you spend eternity?

- Transformation - This world is in self-destruct mode with millions of hopeless, unhappy, discontented people. Millionaires who commit suicide, movie stars who are never content and never have enough money, lovers, or peace. NFL superstars who trade their prized superbowl rings for drugs; movie stars who seem to have it all yet resort to drugs, sex and alcohol and even suicide because they cannot find happiness or fulfillment or peace in this life. Millions have found that it is not money or fame that brings happiness, but a true relationship with Jesus Christ that gives peace, purpose, fulfillment and has transformed people from every walk of life. But most importantly, Jesus Christ offers hope to the hopeless in both this life and the next. He alone, offers eternal life in Heaven. Jesus Christ changes lives.
- God is righteous, just and holy. He gives us free choice as to where we want to spend eternity-- with Him or away from Him in Hell. He will not allow any sin in Heaven, therefore we must choose.

- There is only one way to heaven and that is through Jesus Christ. He died for our sins. We must repent of sin and ask Jesus into our hearts and then live for Him.

With the evidences of each one of these and the culmination of them all, they make the Bible supernatural in origin, unique and alone in the Bible's astounding claims and transforming power like nothing else in the entire world when you choose to seek out its claims.

FINAL EXHORTATION

Revelation 22:12 (NASB)
"Behold, I am coming quickly, and My reward is with Me,
to render to every man according to what he has done. I
am the Alpha and the Omega, the first and the last, the
beginning and the end."

So much is at stake. Ten thousand years from now those of you who accepted Jesus as your Savior will be so glad you did. The Bible is filled with promises to reward those who are faithful to Him as we await and look forward to His coming.

For anyone who does not accept Jesus as their Savior before the rapture, you need to know that End Time events are rapidly drawing closer to the time that the Bible calls 'the Great Tribulation' just before Jesus returns to earth. You will know that you are in the final 3½ to 7 years on earth, because all the true Christians will be gone. This is called the Rapture of the Church. At this point in time it will be extremely difficult to accept Jesus and live for Him. A One-World government, One-World religion, and One-World monetary system will be in place. The Antichrist, (World Dictator) will require allegiance to him and you will be required to take a mark on your right hand or forehead in order to buy or sell. You must not take this mark! This is very serious. Your whole eternity is at stake. You must accept Jesus Christ and give allegiance to Him. These last few years are miniscule compared to all eternity. By this time you will know the Bible is true. If you have waited this long, it will be horrendous days, but it is not too late. Don't pass this last opportunity for Heaven! It is your last.

God keeps His promises and soon He will come back for those who are ready to meet Him. Out of God's great love and desire for you to spend eternity with Him, He is patient in coming back to get us as He tells us in His letter to us, the Bible:

2 Peter 3:3-15 (NASB)
Know this first of all, that in the last days mockers will come with {their} mocking, following after their own lusts, and saying, "Where is the promise of His coming? For {ever} since the fathers fell asleep, all continues just as it was from the beginning of creation." For when they maintain this, it escapes their notice that by the word of God {the} heavens existed long ago and {the} earth was formed out of water and by water, through which the world at that time was destroyed, being flooded with water. But by His word the present heavens and earth are being reserved for fire, kept for the day of judgment and destruction of ungodly men. But do not let this one {fact} escape your notice, beloved, that with the Lord one day is like a thousand years, and a thousand years like one day. The Lord is not slow about His promise, as some count slowness, but is patient toward you, not wishing for any to perish but for all to come to repentance. But the day of the Lord will come like a thief, in which the heavens will pass away with a roar and the elements will be destroyed with intense heat, and the earth and its works will be burned up. Since all these things are to be destroyed in this way, what sort of people ought you to be in holy conduct and

145

godliness, looking for and hastening the coming of the day of God, because of which the heavens will be destroyed by burning, and the elements will melt with intense heat! But according to His promise we are looking for new heavens and a new earth, in which righteousness dwells. Therefore, beloved, since you look for these things, be diligent to be found by Him in peace, spotless and blameless, and regard the patience of our Lord {as} salvation.

And so we see, the reason God is patient in coming back is because He does not want anyone to perish, but He is coming back and the signs show it will be soon. Be sure you are ready to meet Him, so that when you see Him face to face, He will be able to say to you, "Well done, my good and faithful servant."[1]

Appendix 1
Recommended Resources

1. Bibles and Recommended Reading
Good sources: Amazon, CBD. www.CBD, Borders
   A. New King James Nelson Study Bible
   B. The End Time Believers' Evidence Bible compiled by Ray Comfort
   C. Why I Believe by D. James Kennedy
   D. Y-Origins, Back to the Beginning by Chapman, James and Stanford
   E. Y-JESUS, Who was the Real Jesus? by Chapman, James and Stanford
   F. Holman QuickSource Guide to Christian Apologetics by Doug Powell

2. Internet
See listed websites in chapter 6 as well as:
   A. American Scientific Affiliation, asa.calvin.edu
   B. Google "Archaeology"
   C. Reasons to Believe, www.reasons.org
   D. Christian Apologetics, www.carm.org
   E. Y-Origins, www.y-origins.com
   F. Institute for Creation Research, www.icr.org
   G. New believers–www.KnowGodpersonally.org
   H. Christian Book Distributors-www.CBD (Good source for Christian books and supplies.

Appendix 2
Which Religion is Right?
Where Do We Look to Find the Truth?

Why believe in Christianity over all other religions?

The following article, "Why Believe in Christianity over all other religions" (next four pages) is written entirely by Rev. Matthew J.Slick, Copyright 2003, and is used by permission.

Religions contradict each other; therefore, they cannot all be true.

Mormonism teaches that there are many gods in existence and that you can become a god. Christianity teaches that there is only one God and you cannot become a god. Islam teaches that Jesus is not God in flesh where Christianity does. Jesus cannot be both God and not God at the same time. Some religions teach that we reincarnate while others do not. Some teach there is a hell and others do not. They cannot all be true. If they cannot all be true, it cannot be true that all religions lead to God. Furthermore, it means that some religions are, at the very least, false in their claims to reveal the true God (or gods). Remember, truth does not contradict itself. If God exists, He will not institute mutually exclusive and contradictory belief systems in an attempt to get people to believe in Him. God is not the author of confusion (1 Cor. 14:33). Therefore, it is reasonable to believe that there can be an absolute spiritual truth and that not all systems can be true regardless of whether or not they claim to be true. There must be more than a mere claim.

The Bible, Fact or Fiction?

Fulfilled Prophecy concerning Jesus

Though there are other religions that that have prophecies in them, none are 100% accurate as is the Bible and none of them point to someone like Jesus who made incredible claims and performed incredible deeds. The Old Testament was written hundreds of years before Jesus was born. Yet, the Old Testament prophesied many things about Jesus. This is undoubtedly evidence of divine influence upon the Bible.

Please consider some of the many prophecies of Jesus in the following chart.

Prophecy	Old Testament Prophecy	New Test. Fulfillment
Born of a virgin	Isaiah 7:14	Matt. 1:18,25
Born at Bethlehem	Micah 5:2	Matt. 2:1
Rejected by His own people	Isaiah 53:3	John 7:5; 7:48
Betrayed by a close friend	Psalm 41:9	John 13:26-30
His side pierced	Zech. 12:10	John 19:34
Crucifixion	Psalm 22:1, Psalm 22:11-18	Luke 23:33; John 19:23-24
Resurrection of Christ	Psalm 16:10	Acts 13:34-37

The Claims and Deeds of Christ

Christianity claims to be authored by God. Of course, merely making such a claim does not make it true. Anyone can make claims. But, backing up those claims is entirely different. Jesus used the Divine Name for Himself (John 8:58), the same Divine Name used by God when Moses asked God what His name was in (Exodus 3:14). Jesus said that He could do whatever He saw God the Father do (John 5:19), and He claimed to be one with God the Father (John 10:30; 10:38). Likewise, the disciples also called Him God (John 1:1,14; John 10:27; Col. 2:9). By default, if Jesus is God in flesh,

150

then whatever He said and did would be true. Since Jesus said that He alone was the way, the truth, and the life and that no one can find God without Him (John 14:6), this all becomes incredibly important.

Again, making a claim is one thing. Backing it up is another. Did Jesus also back up His words with His deeds? Yes, He did.

- *Jesus changed water into wine (John 2:6-10).*
- *Jesus cast out demons (Matt. 8:28-32; 15:22-28).*
- *Jesus healed lepers (Matt. 8:3; Luke 17:14).*
- *Jesus healed diseases (Matt. 4:23,24; Luke 6:17-19*
- *Jesus healed the paralytic (Mark 2:3-12).*
- *Jesus raised the dead (Matt. 9:25; John 11:43-44).*
- *Jesus restored sight to the blind (Matt. 9:27-30; John 9:1-7).*
- *Jesus restored cured deafness (Mark 7:32-35).*
- *Jesus fed the multitude (Matt. 14:15-21; Matt. 15:32-38).*
- *Jesus walked on water (Matt. 8:26-27).*
- *Jesus calmed a storm with a command (Matt. 8:22-27; Mark 4:39).*
- *Jesus rose from the dead (Luke 24:39; John 20:27).*
- *Jesus appeared to disciples after resurrection (John 20:19).*

The eyewitnesses recorded the miracles of Jesus and the gospels have been reliably transmitted to us. Therefore, we can believe what Jesus said about Himself because Jesus performed many convincing miracles in front of people who testified and wrote about what they saw Him do.

Christ's Resurrection

Within Christianity, the resurrection is vitally important. Without the resurrection, our faith is useless (1 Cor. 15:14). It was the resurrection that changed the lives of the disciples. After Jesus was crucified, the disciples ran and hid. But when they saw the risen Lord, they knew that all that Jesus had said and done proved that He was indeed God in flesh, the Savior.

The Bible, Fact or Fiction?

No other religious leader has died in full view of trained executioners, had a guarded tomb, and then risen three days later to appear to many people. This resurrection is proof of who Jesus is and that He did accomplish what He set out to do: provide redemption for mankind.

Buddha did not rise from the dead. Muhammad did not rise from the dead. Confucius did not rise from the dead. Krishna did not rise from the dead, etc. Only Jesus has physically risen from the dead, walked on water, claimed to be God, and raised others from the dead. He has conquered death. Why trust anyone else? Why trust anyone who can be held by physical death when we have a Messiah who is greater than death itself?

Why should anyone trust in Christianity over Islam, Buddhism, Mormonism, or anything else? It is because there are absolute truths, because only in Christianity is there accurate fulfilled prophecies of a coming Messiah. Only in Christianity do we have the extremely accurate transmission of the eyewitness documents (gospels) so we can trust what was originally written. Only in Christianity do we have the person of Christ who claimed to be God, performed many miracles to prove His claim of divinity, who died and rose from the dead, and who said that He alone was the way the truth and the life. All this adds to the legitimacy and credibility of Christianity above all other religions -- all based on the person of Jesus. It follows that if it is all true about what Jesus said and did, then all other religions are false because Jesus said that He alone was the way, the truth, and the life and that no one comes to the Father except through Him (John 14:6). It could not be that Jesus is the only way and truth and other religions also be the truth. Either Jesus is true and all other religions are false or other religions are true and Jesus is false. There are no other options. I choose to follow the risen Lord. (The above article, *Why Believe in Christianity over other Religions,* www.carm.org *was used by permission.)*

Before we go into the basic beliefs of the world's major religions it is important to note that all the great religious teachers, leaders and prophets who ever lived **never** made the claims that Jesus did, and not one of them is equal to him. Consider the following: Confucius, Buddha, Lao Tze, never claimed to be anything but sinful men. Mohammed and Joseph Smith were unable to show proofs that they were true prophets of God. None of them claimed what Jesus does. In the *Koran* the Muslim prophet Mohammed states, "Muhammad is naught but a messenger" and "Surely I am no more than a human apostle."[1] In fact, several times in *The Koran,* Mohammed who is acknowledged as sinful, asks forgiveness from God, or is even rebuked by God. (From The Koran, J.M. Rodwell, Tans pp 244, 384, 423,460,468, etc. Sura 4:106; 40:57; 47:21; 48:2; 110:3)[2] Note the big difference – Mohammed said he was sinful, but Jesus claimed he was sinless. Mohammed only claimed to be a prophet but Jesus claimed to be God. What about Buddha? Buddha just said he was an enlightened man who could show others the way to "nirvana" a state of personal dissolution in the afterlife. He repeatedly insisted he was human in every respect and made no attempt to conceal his temptations and weaknesses. What did Confucius say? "As to being a Divine Sage or even a Good Man, far be it for me to make any such claim." (Taken from The Analects of Confucius, Arthur Way, trans, 1938, p. 130) Confucius stated he was neither divine nor even a good man, whereas Jesus claimed He was divine and morally perfect. The important point here to note is that Jesus Christ was able to make such an astounding claim because he could. His purity and morality has stood the test of time when others could have disputed his claims and eagerly would have if they could, but many that knew him, both non-religious and his religious followers attested to the truth of what he claimed. People are always eager to expose lies when they can.

Jesus claimed to be the Son of God, one with God and

the Savior of the world. All the other religions make no such claim. Their leaders were mere men with inadequacies of their own, and only claimed to be prophets, teachers or leaders. Why settle for just a follower rather than Jesus Christ, the Son of God Himself, who is the only way to God the Father and thus to Heaven?

What are the basic beliefs of other religions?

If there is only one way to Heaven as the Bible states, and remembering that the Bible is the only book that contains sciences, history, astronomy, geography and prophecy that is confirmed with complete accuracy, then when it states that the only way to Heaven is through Jesus Christ as opposed to theories and religions that teach different ways, then they all can't be right. So, let's look at what the following main religions and philosophies teach.

It is interesting to note that the earliest accounts of man are found in the Holy Bible. Notice the beginning dates of the main religions:

- Judaism & Christianity – Approx 2000 BC in the Middle East
- Mormonism-1830 in New York
- Jehovah Witness – 1800's in Pennsylvania
- Islam – 622 AD around Mecca
- Buddhism – 563 BC in Nepal and India

- **Hinduism** – Teaches the belief in millions of gods and teaches karma- the total compilation of all a person's past lives and actions that result in the present condition of that person. In other words they believe in reincarnation. The purpose of reincarnation is to allow the individual to learn spiritual lessons through life so he/she may return to God from where the soul came.
- Buddhism – Relates karma directly to motives behind an action. Reincarnation. Among the different beliefs that have developed

through the years Buddhists believe if your karma is good when you die you will come back as a statesman or dignitary, but if your karma is bad, you'll come back as an animal, but then if you're a good animal, you'll come back as a person. They have diversified into many different groups and philosophies so that it is hard to generalize it past Karma. The original teachings of the historical Buddha are extremely difficult, if not impossible, to recover or reconstruct.

- Hindus also believe in Karma. Reincarnation.
- Islam- Founder – Muhammed. Muslim's God is Allah. The Quran describes Allah as khayru al-makireen. Translation: "Allah is the best Deceiver Schemer Conniver."(cf S. 3:54; 8:30) Other names: The Distresser, Afflicter, Punisher, Pride-filled³ Belief: One sure way of getting into heaven is by shedding the blood of infidels (infidels being anyone who is not Muslim.) This is a hateful religion.In a conference I attended recently, Walid Shoebat, a former PLO Muslim terrorist – now a practicing Christian said, "My country has literally become the night of the living dead. If I were to go back there I would be beheaded. Even children are seen walking down streets holding human organs etc. from lynchings of those who rejected Islam." August 2007 (Important Note regarding Islam: There are many in Islam that are radically teaching that everyone who does not practice the belief of the Islam religion are to be killed. These radical Muslims are so strong in their belief that they are murdering hundreds everyday from Israel, America, Britain, Africa and all continents who will not adhere to their belief, this includes the murder of their own family members. Their own documented media promotes this hate and shows video from school age children on up to adults chanting and teaching war games to kill the hated Americans, Israelites, etc. This is very serious! Their immediate goal is to destroy America, Israel and any nation that stands in their way of forcing Islam on the world.)
- Mormonism – Founded by Joseph Smith in 1830 in New York. Mormons believe God was previously a mere man on another planet. (Mormon Doctrine, p. 321) He became a god by following the laws and ordinances of that god on that planet and

came to this world with his wife who became a goddess, and supposedly they produced a spirit offspring in heaven, which includes Jesus, Lucifer (the devil) and you and me, and we are all brothers and sisters born in the preexistence. (Mormons believe that Satan and Jesus are brothers.) Mormons who pay a full 10% tithe of their income to the Mormon church and go through Mormon temples, believe they have the potential of becoming gods of their own planets and are then able to start the procedure over again. Everyone who follows this doctrine has the potential to become a god. Mormons do not tell you that there are numerous secrets in their religion such as celestial marriage, secret temple rituals, baptism of the dead, various oaths of secrecy and commitment. Non-Mormon parents of Mormon couples getting married are not allowed to attend their own children's wedding.

- Jehovah Witnesses – Began in 1876 in Pennsylvania. Founder is Charles Taze Russell who was later joined by Nelson Barbour. Nelson Barbour predicted the visible return of Christ at 1873 and when that failed to occur, he revised the prediction to 1874. Soon after Barbour's second disappointment, his study group decided Christ had returned invisibly to Earth in 1874. In July 1879 Russell and Barbour separated into their own groups. For more information see www.Wikipedia.com. According to Jehovah Witnesses the way most earn everlasting life on earth is by door-to-door work. Salvation in Heaven is limited to 144,000 anointed ones. This number is already reached.

- Wicca /Witchcraft/the Occult/Satanism-All stem from demonic, mystical worship of Satan. Satanists are the new fastest growing subculture among America's teens. Satanists have their own chaplains in the U.S. Armed Forces and are protected under freedom-of-religion laws. The occult world of demonic power, once a terror to most, has become storybook entertainment of the modern world, now sought after as "psychic power". Demonology and wizardry are now being promoted in books, video games, and movies. The negative effects of the magic of wizardry are no longer just read about in fiction, but are the secret ambition of millions of teenagers. From children to adult, millions are being captivated by Harry

Appendix

Potter and numerous sources of the occult.

- Christianity - God created Heaven and earth, the sun, the moon and the stars. He created plant life and animal life, but humanity is God's prize creation. The central theme throughout the Bible is about the love and provision He made for us through His Son, Jesus Christ, in order that we may spend all eternity in fellowship with Him. Although God is powerful enough to make the universe, His great love for all people is central to the Christian belief in that Christianity is about relationship with God, the Creator of everything and everyone. God does not force anyone to love Him. He gives us the choice to either love Him or reject Him, but His desire and purpose for everyone is to spend all eternity with Him.

Photo Credits

NASA
Introduction
Ib. NASA source:http//history.nasa.gov/ap08fj/photots/a/as08-16-2493.jpg
Chapters
1b. Hubblesite/Gallery/Spiral Galaxy M100
1c. Galaxy- NASA/Hubble Gallery, ESA, S. Beckwith (STScI), and The
    Hubble Heritage Team (STScI/AURA)
1g. NASA/Goddard Space Flight Center
1h. Image Credit: European Space Agency & NASA Acknowledgment: E.
    Olszewski (University of Arizona)
6D. PD-USGov-NASA

WIKIMEDIA COMMONS
Pictures under this section are in the Public Domain and are distributed &
licensed under GFDL. See "http://www.gnu.org/copyleft/fdl.html" In short;
you are free to share and make derivative works **of the photo** under the
conditions that you appropriately attribute it, and that you distribute it only
under a license identical to this one.
Introduction
Ia. Nuclear Test/Wikipedia;
    http://upload.wikimedia.org/wikpedia/commons/c/c9/Nuclear_Fireball.j
    pg, Alternative Source:
    http://www.nv.doe.gov/library/photos/photodetails.aspx US Gov. PD
Chapter 1
1a. Earth and Mars/Wikimedia Commons. PD. Credit: JPL/NASA
    Source: http://photojournal.jpl.nasa.gov/catalog/PIA02570
1d. Earth's Tilt-Wikimedia Commons/Earth Tilt/I, Dennis Nilsson, the
    copyright holder of this work, has published or hereby publishes it
    under the following under the Creative Commons Attribution License.
    Source:
    http://upload.wikimedia.org/wikipedial/commons/6/61/AxialTiltObliqu
    ity.png
1e. Moon-Wikimedia Commons. Public Domain Source:

The Bible, Fact or Fiction?

http//www.photolib.noaa.gov/coastline/line0510.htm

1f. Skyscraper – Wikimedia Commons, Image: Bank of China night.jpg; self photographed; September 2001 by User:Filzstift. Permission is granted to copy, distribute and/or modify this document under the terms of the GNU Free Documentation License, Version 1.2 or any later version.

1i. Brain – Wikimedia Commons/Cerebral - Source: Government http://www.toosmarttostart.samhsa.gov/InteractiveBody/html/cerebral.htm

1j. Eye – Wikimedia Commons/Human Eye/Public Domain.No author given

1k. Heart – Wikimedia Commons/Image:Aorta.jpg, the copyright holder of this work, hereby release it into the public domain.

Chapter 2

2a. Ape – Wikimedia Commons/ US Fed. Government. PD Source: www.usaid.gov/cg/photobonobo.html

2b. Fish – Wikimedia/Rainbow Fish/PD/US Fish and Wildlife Service, US Gov.

2c. Wikimedia Commons/Birds in Flight-PD US Government, http://images.fws.gov/defarult.cfm?fuseaction+records.display

2d. Elephant-Wikimedia Commons, PD, Author: Rworsnop at the English Wikipedia project.

2e. Frog-Wikipedia/Tree Frog; PD by Author:LiquidGhoul

2f. King Arthur/Wikimedia; PD Expired copyright.

2g. Jets/Wikipedia; PD, Author:Yussef90@the Wikipedia Project

2h. Tornado/Wikimedia Commons; www.spc.noaa.gov/faq/tornado/torscan.htm

2i. Architect//Wikipedia; PD, expired copyright.

Chapter 3

3a.. Israel Map/Wikimedia Commons; PD, NASA

3b. Smithsonian/Wikimedia Commons; PD, Author Noclip.

3c. Manuscript/Wikimedia Commons; PD, Expired Copyright

3d. Pontius Pilate/Wikimedia Commons:PD, Expired Copyright, Source: http://en.wikipedia.org/wiki/Image:Eccehomo1.jpg

Chapter 4

4a. Bible/Wikimedia Commons/Holy Bible; Beinecke-gutenberg Bible;PD, picture taken by Henry Trotter.

Chapter 5

5a. US Currency Federal Reserve/Wikimedia Commons. PD. US Government http://www.hd.org/Damon/photos/money/archive-7.HTM

5b.Iran Map/Wikipedia; PD. Expired Copyright. Author: William

Photo Credits

Shepherd. Source
http://www.lib.utexas.edu/maps/historical/shepherd/persian_empire.jpg
5c. Algebra Class/Wikipedia, PD. Author: Tungsten
5d. Scale/en Wikipedia, PD, US GOV-DOE
5e. Resurrection/Wikimedia Commons, PD, reproduction of the Yorck
   Project.Compilation copyright is held by Zenodot Verlagsgesellschaft
   mbh and licensed under the GNU Free Documentation license.
5f. Jesus/Wikipedia, PD. Expired Copyright. Source:
   www.museodelprado.es/uploads/tx_gbobras/po1167a 01f2004.jpg
5g. News/Wikimedia Commons, PD.
   Source:http://openclipart./clipart//unsorted/newspaper_aubanel_monnie
   _01.svg
5h. Greek Architecture/Wikimedia Commons, PD,Expired copyright. This
   file has been extracted from an original image in *The New Student's
   Reference Work*: File:LA2-NSRW-1-0122.jpg
5i. Easter Bunny/Wikipedia; PD, Expired Copyright, Author: ItsLassieTime
5j. Josephus Flavius/Wikimedia Commons, PD. Expired copyright
   Source http://en.wikipedia.org/wiki/Image:Josephus.jpg, Author: John
   Winston

Chapter 6
6a. Sunset/Wikimedia Commons, PD. Author: M. Buschmann
6b. Israel Newspaper/Wikimedia Commons, PD. Expired copyright.
   Source Scan. Originally from en.wikipedia. Original uploader was
   Humus sapiens at en.wikipedia.
6c. Nascar/Wikimedia Commons, Author U.S. Air Force photo by Larry
   McTighe
6e. Irish Jaunting/Wikipedia, PD, Expired
   Copyright.http://hdl.loc.gov/loc.pnp/ppmsc.09947
6f. Nuclear Test/Wikimedia Commons, PD. US Federal Government
   Alt.Source:http://www.nv.doe.gov/library/photos/photodetails.aspx?ID
   =1048
6g. US Currency Federal Reserve/Wikimedia Commons. PD. US
   Government http://www.hd.org/Damon/photos/money/archive-7.HTM
6h. Rfid/Wikimedia Commons, Photo of Amal Graafstra, a Washington
   state native and business owner, having an RFID chip implanted in his
   left hand in early 2005. Photo from
   http://flickr.com/photos/28129213@N00/7267161/in/set-181299/This
   photo was taken just after the operation to insert the RFID tag was
   completed. This file is licensed under Creative Commons Attribution
   ShareAlike 2.0
6i. Sky/Wikimedia Commons, Opis, PD

Chapter 7

7a. Creation/Wikimedia Commons, PD.Expired copyright. Creation of Light, by en:Gustave Doré.

7b. Creation/Wikimedia Commons, PD, Author: Anthony 5429, Source: http://upload.wikimedia.org/wikipedia/commons/7/78/Creation_Museu m_7.png

Notes

Chapter 1
1. D. James Kennedy, *Why I Believe*, (W Publishing Group, 1980, 1999), Coral Ridge Ministries, www.CoralRidge.org, 33
2. Ibid., p. 33, 34
3. Ibid., p.34
4. Ibid., p. 35
5. Ibid., p. 36
6. Ibid., p. 36
7. H.M.S. Richards, Jr., *Fireworks in the Sky*, (Washington DC: Review and Herald Publishing Association, 1988) 22-24
8. D. James Kennedy, *Why I Believe*, (Waco, Texas: Word Books, 1984) 46
9. Larry Chapman, Rick James and Eric Stanford, *Back to the Beginning, Y-Origins*, (Bright Media Foundation and B&L Publications, 2004), www.y-origins.com, 78-81
10. D. James Kennedy, *Why I Believe*, 1984, 46
11. Larry Chapman, Rick James and Eric Stanford, *Back to the Beginning, Y-Origins*, 2004, 41
12. Doug Powell, *Holman QuickSource Guide to Christian Apologetics,*(Nashville, Tennessee: Holman Reference, 2006), B&H Publishing Group used by permission, 66
13. D. James, Kennedy, *Why I Believe*, 1984, 45

Chapter 2
1. Ray Comfort, *The End Time Believer's Evidence Bible*, (Gainsville, Florida: Bridge-Logos, 2003), 1421
2. Robert W. Faid, *A Scientific Approach to Christianity*, used with permission from current publisher New Leaf Publishing Group, Green Forest, AR, c 1982, 113
3. Ibid., 112
4. Grant Jeffrey quote, The Signature of God
5. Chapman, James and Stanford, *Back to the Beginning– Y-Origins*, (Bright Media Foundation and B&L Publications, 2004), 68
6. Henry Morris, *Many Infallible Proofs*, (San Diego, California: Creation-

Life Books, 1984), used by permission by current publisher, New Leaf Publishing Group, Green Forest, AR, 255

7. Ray Comfort, *The End Time Believer's Evidence Bible*, 2003, 769

Chapter 3
1. Henry Morris, *Many Infallible Proofs*, (San Diego, California: Creation-Life Books1984), used by permission by current publisher, New Leaf Publishing Group, Green Forest, AR, 46
2. Ibid., 47
3. D. James Kennedy, *Why I Believe* (Waco, Texas: Word Books, 1984) www.CoralRidge.org, 30
4. Ibid., 31
5. Ibid., 31-32
6. Robert Faid, *A Scientific Approach to Christianity*, (South Plainfield, New Jersey: Bridge Publishing, 1982), used with permission from current publisher New Leaf Publishing Group, Green Forest, AR 43
7. Ibid., 45
8. Lee Strobel, *The Case for Christ*, (Grand Rapids, Michigan: Zondervan 1998,) 107
9. Robert Faid, *A Scientifc Approach to Christianity*, 44
10. D. James Kennedy, *Why I Believe*, 1999, 103
11. Chapman, James, Stanford, Y-Jesus, *Who was the Real Jesus?*, 12
12. Ibid., 9

Chapter 4 – Reliability of the Scriptures
1. Matthew J. Slick, *Christian Apologetic & Research Ministry Notebook*, 2003, www.carm.org, 381
2. Robert W. Faid, *A Scientific Approach to Christianity*, (South Plainfield, New Jersey: Bridge Publishing, 1982), used with permission from current publisher New Leaf Publishing Group, Green Forest, AR, 19-20
3. Chart is adapted from two sources: www.carm.org, Matthew Slick by Norman Geisler, 1976 p. 307; Josh McDowell and Bill Wilson, *A Ready Defense*, Nashville, Tennese: Thomas Nelson, Inc.1993) 45.
4. Matthew Slick Christian Apologetic & Research, www.carm.org, 2007,
5. Josh McDowell and Don Stewart, *Answers to Tough Questions*, (Tyndale House Publishers, 1980), www.josh.org, 19

Chapter 5 Prophetical Evidences
1. Larry Chapman, Rick James, Eric Stanford, *Who Was the Real Jesus? Y-Jesus*, (Bright Media Foundation and B &L Publications, 2006), www.y-origins. Com, 59

Notes

2. Ibid., 59
3. D. James Kennedy, *Why I Believe*, (Waco, Texas: Word Books,1999), www. CoralRidge.org, 3-4
4. Ibid., 2
5. Chapman, James and Stanford, *Who Was the Real Jesus?*, 61
6. D. James Kennedy, *Why I Believe*, 1999, 130
7. Ibid., 130
8. Ibid., 130,131
9. Chapman, James and Stanford, *Who Was the Real Jesus?*, 73
10. Ibid., 75
11. Ibid., 76
12. Ibid., 77
13. D. James Kennedy, *Why I Believe* 1999, 132
14. Ibid., 132, 133
15. Ibid., 106

Chapter 7 Choices

1. D. James Kennedy, *Why I Believe*, 1999, 151-152
2. Ibid., 152
3. Josh McDowell, *Christianity Hoax or History?* (Wheaten, Illinois: Tyndale House Publishers, 1989), www.josh.org, 66
4. Josh McDowell and Don Stewart, *Answers to Tough Questions*, (San Bernadino, California: Here's Life Publishers, 1980) 62-63
5. New American Standard Bible, (Grand Rapids, Michigan: Zondervan Publishing House, 1999) Romans 5:8

Chapter 8 – In a Nutshell

1. Matthew 25:21

Appendix 2 Which Religion is Right?

1. John Ankerberg & John Weldon, *Knowing the Truth about Salvation*, 1997 by the John Ankerberg Show, Published by Harvest House Publishers, Eugene, Oregon, used by permission, www.harvesthousepublishers.com. 28
2. Ibid., 28
3. Google "Koran" www.welcometothenglishtranslationof theKoran

To order more copies of the book
The Bible, Fact or Fiction?
Log on to
www.outskirtspress.com/thebiblefactorfiction

Accompanying Workbook also available January 2010 for those interested in personal or group study.

To order workbooks email:
evidencefortruth@yahoo.com

LaVergne, TN USA
30 October 2009

162629LV00002B/1/P